U0565235

本书编写组 编

中华优秀传统文化书系

Excellent Chinese Traditional Culture
The Works of Mencius

孟子

（一）

山东画报出版社

图书在版编目（CIP）数据

孟子／本书编写组编. —济南：山东画报出版社，2020.8
（中华优秀传统文化书系）

ISBN 978-7-5474-3653-0

Ⅰ.①孟⋯ Ⅱ.①本⋯ Ⅲ.①儒家 ②《孟子》—注释 ③《孟子》—译文 Ⅳ.①B222.5

中国版本图书馆CIP数据核字（2020）第104723号

中华优秀传统文化书系：孟子

本书编写组 编

项目策划	梁济生
项目统筹	秦　超
责任编辑	姜　辉　梁培培
特邀编辑	仇　雨　张嘉奥
装帧设计	李海峰

出　版　人	李文波
主管单位	山东出版传媒股份有限公司
出版发行	山东画报出版社
社　　址	济南市市中区英雄山路189号B座　邮编 250002
电　　话	总编室（0531）82098472
	市场部（0531）82098479　82098476（传真）
网　　址	http：//www.hbcbs.com.cn
电子信箱	hbcb@sdpress.com.cn
印　　刷	山东星海彩印有限公司
规　　格	787毫米×1000毫米　1/32
	42.5印张　39幅图　600千字
版　　次	2020年8月第1版
印　　次	2020年8月第1次印刷
书　　号	ISBN 978-7-5474-3653-0
定　　价	272.00元（全四册）

如有印装质量问题，请与出版社总编室联系更换。

出版说明

　　山东是儒家文化的发源地，也是中华优秀传统文化的重要发祥地，在灿烂辉煌的中华传统文化"谱系"中占有重要地位。用好齐鲁文化资源丰富的优势，扎实推进中华优秀传统文化研究阐发、保护传承和传播交流，推动中华优秀传统文化创造性转化、创新性发展，是习近平总书记对山东提出的重大历史课题、时代考卷，也是山东坚定文化自信、守护中华民族文化根脉的使命担当。

　　为挖掘阐发、传播普及以儒家思想为代表的中华优秀传统文化，推动中华文明与世界不同文明交流互鉴，山东省委宣传部组织策划了"中华优秀传统文化书系",并列入山东省优秀传统文化传承发展工程重点项目。书系以儒家经典"四书"(《大学》《中庸》《论语》《孟子》)为主要内容,对儒家文化蕴含的哲学思想、人文精神、教化思想、道德理念等进行了现代性阐释。书系采用权威底本、精心校点、审慎译注,同时添加了权威英文翻译和精美插图,是兼具历史性与时代性、民族性与国际性、学术性与普及性、艺术性与实用性于一体的精品佳作。

前　言

　　《孟子》是记录孟子及其弟子言行以及孟子游说各国国君、同各派思想家进行辩论的语录体著作。它集中反映了孟子的思想体系，同时保留了不少战国时期的历史信息，为我们理解孟子、走进百家争鸣那个时代提供了基本材料。

一、孟子其人其书

　　孟子，名轲，战国时期邹（今山东邹城）人。相传孟子是鲁国贵族孟孙氏后裔，幼年丧父，家庭贫穷，迁居至邹，由其母抚养长大。

孟子是继孔子、曾子、子思之后儒家学派又一位重要人物，被后世誉为"亚圣"，与孔子并称"孔孟"。其生卒年不见详载，杨伯峻考证为约公元前385年到公元前304年。孟子在书中说："予未得为孔子徒也，予私淑诸人也。"孟子以继承孔子衣钵为己任，但未能言明其师是何人。关于孟子之师，学界有所争论，但多以《史记·孟子荀卿列传》所载为是，即"受业子思之门人"，也就是说孟子是孔子的孙子——子思的再传弟子，可谓是儒门正宗。所以其书以继承发扬孔子的思想为要，正所谓"退而与万章之徒序《诗》《书》，述仲尼之意，作《孟子》七篇"。

《孟子》的主要内容来源于孟子自是无疑，可其具体作者，学界有不同认识，比如孟子自著；孟子门下弟子万章和公孙丑之徒在孟子死后所著等，其中以在孟子生前由弟子辅助所著最能为人接受。《史记》记载《孟子》为七篇，而应劭《风俗通义·穷通篇》

却说："退与万章之徒序《诗》《书》，仲尼之意，作书中、外十一篇。"《汉书·艺文志》也著录"《孟子》十一篇"。赵岐以《外书》四篇为伪，故不为之作注，后世研读者日少，逐渐亡佚。到了明代，姚士粦又伪撰《孟子外书》四篇，清人周广业指斥其"显属伪托"，梁启超则以其为"伪中出伪"。

《孟子》七篇，每篇分上下，计十四卷二百六十章，总计三万五千余字，是"四书"中部头最大、内容最丰富的一本。但长期以来《孟子》一直处于子书或传文位置，直到五代十国时期后蜀诏刻十一经将其列入，后宋太宗加以翻刻，《孟子》才开始进入经书行列。到南宋朱熹把《论语》《大学》《中庸》《孟子》合刊编写《四书章句集注》，《孟子》更加受到学者重视，孟子的思想也更大程度上影响了中国古代思想史的进程。

二、《孟子》之思想

　　《孟子》一书思想宏大、细致入微，主要反映了孟子本人及其同时代人的人性论、政治思想，以及孟子本人独特的经济思想、生态观、工夫论，其中涵盖了其与时人的义利（欲）之辩、人禽之辩、性命之辩、心体之辩等诸多内容。但由于其语录体的展开形式，孟子的同一思想多散落到各篇的许多章中，我们在理解的时候要仔细爬梳，把同一主题的全部相关内容放到一起进行综合判断，而不能一叶障目、断章取义。

　　人性论　　人性论是先秦诸子乃至整个中国思想史的核心论题，孟子的人性论更是其思想体系的出发点和终极依据。孟子的人性论是通过其与告子的辩论展开的，主要见于《告子上》一篇。告子认为"性无善无不善"，其时还有人认为"性可以为善，可以为不善"，后来荀子则力主性恶论，与此相对，孟子的人性论为性善论。这些都是继孔子"性相近"之后的不同阐发路径。

孟子"性善论"之"性"是指人之异于禽兽的"几希"之性，而不是作为实然起点的与生俱来的性的全部；其"善"则是指道德意义上的正向发挥。孟子证明性善是通过心善来完成的，以心善言性善，即本心在摆脱生理欲望后自主呈现的善，是人之所以为人的道德主体，是性善的根本依据。所以其有涵盖恻隐之心、羞恶之心、恭敬之心、是非之心的"四心"说，并以此四心为仁、义、礼、智四德之端，由此说明"四心""四德"皆"非由外铄我也，我固有之也"。需要注意的是孟子并不认为四德是齐一的，而仍是以"仁"为统领的。既然性是善的，那恶又从何而来？孟子认为人受于耳目物欲之蔽而丧失其本心，恶由是而生。告子认为"食色性也"，但孟子认为耳目之欲一类虽从与生俱来意义上是为性的，而从其实现意义上则取决于外，是

有命的，故人的本心是会被物欲所蔽而最终
失于流放的，所以"君子不谓性也"。既然
恶能产生，我们又当如何处理呢？

　　孟子提出"求其放心"的方法论。"放心"
就是被物欲"引之"而流失的本心，若要回
归本性之善，必须找回此"放心"，使其复
如原态。此一过程全由人的自觉意识和自主
行动主宰，所以孟子的性善论既是对人的价
值的肯定，也推动了人主体自由的崛起和心
灵自主的实现，正如其所说"万物皆备于我"，
以及"舍我其谁"的自信精神。

　　性情关系是孟子人性论的又一重要论述，
"乃若其情，则可以为善矣，乃所谓善也"，
其意为情理并非经验，应然未必实然，价值
根源于主体自觉，实现价值的能力就在性善
的本质之中。孟子的人性论是和天命论相伴
而行的，其内在逻辑为"尽其心者，知其性也；
知其性，则知天矣"。由此而衍生出"存其心，
养其性，所以事天也"的工夫论。

工夫论 孟子的工夫论可以概括为：存心、养性、集义、养浩然之气。存心、养性皆直接出自其性善论，前文已交代明白，此处，外加一条便是防范本心之失的根本措施——寡欲。

孟子极为注重集义，不仅与告子进行义内义外的辩论，而且直言"礼门义路"，把践行仁义作为人生唯一的根本正途。由集义而生养浩然之气，浩然之气至大至刚，就是"集义所生者"。人性是善的，但社会环境是复杂的，环境的复杂极易导致人性背离本善，所以人人皆需时刻自持。总之，孟子的工夫论就是保养其性善论的方法论，就是扩充四端的根本要求。

政治思想 孟子的政治思想是其思想体系的致用主体部分，也是先秦各家政治思想中的巅峰之作。如萧公权《中国政治思想史》所说："孟子之政治思想遂成为针对虐政之永久抗议。"孟子直接继承孔子"苛政猛于虎"

的批判，针对"民之憔悴于虐政"的现实情况，孟子把孔子仁的思想具体发展成为切于时弊的仁政思想。孟子仁政思想的巨大贡献在于其扭转了政治思想中的君民关系，把统治者为政治意志统领的位置转变为一切以人民的意志为根据，统治者遂沦为政治的执行者，而人民成为真正的政治归属，即民本思想。

孟子的"民为贵，社稷次之，君为轻"一语道破玄机，成为中国历代君王头上那把高悬的民意之剑。遵循民意也就成了统治者行事的根本出发点，必得以民"所欲与之聚之，所恶勿施尔也"，也就是《梁惠王下》中所说的"国人杀之"。如果统治者不以民意行事，甚至为国作乱、恣意施政，那该怎么处理呢？孟子对此提出了政权转移的学说。齐宣王以为"汤放桀，武王伐纣"是弑君行为，而孟子却说："贼仁者谓之贼，贼义者谓之残，残贼之人谓之一夫。闻诛一夫纣矣，未闻弑君也。"可见君之为君必得践行仁义，而不能戕害仁义、祸乱百姓，否则君便不再称其君，人人可取而代之。但此一政权转移说被历代统治者解释、执行为双重标准：一方面，在取代上一政权时，批判其违背民意而被自己取代；另一方面，到王朝后期，政治日渐腐败时，自己则对此说讳莫如深。基于此说，孟子在游说各国君主时，常常劝其施行仁政、招揽人心，此所谓"王道"（"王天下"之道）。

由仁政，孟子还提出了与之相关的具体措施，其中蕴含了与民养教、发展经济、保护生态等特色内容。"先王有不忍人之心，斯有不忍人之政矣"，王者要有"天下有溺者，由己溺之也……天下有饥者，由己饥之也"的同情之心，以及在此同情之心的基础上发展出"解民于倒悬"的"不忍人之政"。民众的幸福首先来自生活的富足，所以孟子提出"制民之产"，提出"五亩之宅，树之以桑""鸡豚狗彘之畜，无失其时""百亩之田，勿夺其时""谨庠序之教，申之以孝悌之义"的养教措施。只要统治者肯认真施行，则"黎民不饥不寒""民养生丧死无憾也"，进而民有所恒产，"有恒产者有恒心"，也就避免了"无恒产者无恒心。苟无恒心，放辟邪侈，无不为已"的混乱局面，如此也就不会"不王"了。

孟子的经济思想进而衍生出了生态保护的思想，即"数罟不入洿池""斧斤以时入山林"，虽然很难说孟子自主意识里保护自然的思想是成熟的，但这种朴素的主张确实有其重要历史意义。而且孟子经济思想中还兼顾农、工、商诸业。对于农业，他构建了理想化的"井田制"（无论井田制在孟子之前是否施行过，孟子提出的井田制都是一种土地改革意愿式的理想化主张）；对于工商业，他提出"关，市讥而不征""市，廛而不征，法而不廛"，使其自由发展而不设限。孟子的政治思想博大精深，在战国时期诸侯争霸的时代背景中可谓是一股清流，但其"贵王贱霸"的主张和诸侯国君的利益诉求背道而驰，常被认为是"迂远而阔于事情"，终未被接受和施行，而其在思想史上却具有深远意义，对后世为政者的警醒和对民众的养教也有着不可磨灭的历史贡献。

我们分析孟子思想体系时，尤需注意孟子的人文关怀、现实关怀，注意其以继承发扬孔子思想为己任的使命感，注意其发先圣所未发的创新点，注意其针对"邪说"加以批驳的责任感。其论说多有所指，而非是"好辩"而已。其说："杨墨之道不息，孔子之道不著，是邪说诬民，充塞仁义也。"

三、七篇贻矩，惠及今日

清雍正皇帝手书"七篇贻矩"金匾，悬挂于山东邹城孟府大堂檐下正中，向人们昭示着孟子著书的伟大功绩和对后世的惠及之恩。本书能将两千多年前孟子的著述再次呈现给读者，并把其中的思想价值进行现代化阐释，也是我们承担历史接续的光荣。

《孟子》的历史价值　孔子罕言性与命，到子思则大论性命，到了孟子更是把儒家性命论推向了高峰，所以学界有"思孟学派"一说。这一性命论不仅参与了先秦诸子的历史讨论，还直接影响了宋明以来程朱理学、陆王心学的此起彼伏。孟子的政治思想虽未能在当时施行，但其理论进步意义远高于当时指导兼并战争的"合纵连横"思想，而且孟子反对战争，认为"春秋无义战"。孟子的仁政思想其实不是简单的民本主义，其内在确实含有近代民主主义的色彩。自秦以降，中国历代都没能很好地执行孟子政治思想中最为根本的积极因素，甚至某些时候与之背道而驰，与孟子思想比照起来可以说是一种历史的倒退。孟子在其思想中呈现出的伟岸人格为历代读书人所景仰，孟子思想中的永恒意义一直照耀着我们前行的道路。

《孟子》的现实价值　孟子距今已两千

余载，但其思想时刻浮现在我们脑海，其教诲始终萦绕于我们耳边。继承孟子思想是我们的历史责任，发扬孟子哲学是我们的时代使命，所以我们必须深入理解孟子思想，解剖其实质内涵，辨析其根本，进而完成其创造性转化，通过实践使之得到创新性发展。回望身后，其实也照耀着前方的路。孟子思想体系中的积极因素，既有着进行历史研究、哲学研究、政治研究、社会研究的重大学术价值，也有着指导当下实践、启发政治生活、警醒不良之风的实际意义。而这些意义的实现前提是我们要立足当下，科学把握孟子思想，真正把《孟子》读好、读透。

Contents

梁惠王上

1.1

孟子见梁惠王[1]。王曰："叟[2]不远千里而来，亦将有以利吾国乎？"

孟子对曰："王何必曰利？亦[3]有仁义而已矣。王曰：'何以利吾国？'大夫曰：'何以利吾家？'士庶人曰：'何以利吾身？'上下交征[4]利而国危矣。万乘[5]之国弑[6]其君者，必千乘之家；千乘之国弑其君者，必百乘之家。万取千焉，千取百焉，不为不多矣。苟[7]为后义而先利，不夺不餍[8]。未有仁而遗[9]其亲者也，未有义而后其君者也。王亦曰仁义而已矣，何必曰利？"

Mencius went to see king Hui of Liang. The king said, "Venerable sir, since you have not counted it far to come here, a distance of a thousand *li*, may I presume that you are provided with counsels to profit my kingdom?"

Mencius replied, "Why must Your Majesty use that word 'profit?' What I am provided with, are counsels to benevolence and righteousness, and these are my only topics. If Your Majesty say, 'What is to be done to profit my kingdom?' the great officers will say, 'What is to be done to profit our families?' and the inferior officers and the common people will say, 'What is to be done to profit our persons?' Superiors and inferiors will try to snatch this profit the one from the other, and the kingdom will be endangered. In the kingdom of ten thousand chariots, the murderer of his sovereign shall be the chief of a family of a thousand chariots. In the kingdom of a thousand chariots, the murderer of his prince shall be the chief of a family of a hundred chariots. To have a thousand in ten thousand, and a hundred in a thousand, cannot be said not to be a large allotment, but if righteousness be put last, and profit be put first, they will not be satisfied without snatching all. There never has been a benevolent man who neglected his parents. There never has been a righteous man who made his sovereign an after consideration. Let Your Majesty also say, 'Benevolence and righteousness, and let these be your only themes.' Why must you use that word— 'profit?'"

【注释】［1］梁惠王：就是魏惠王，即位后由安邑迁都大梁，所以又称梁惠王。［2］叟：对老年男人的尊称。［3］亦：这里是"只"的意思。［4］交征：互相争夺。［5］乘（shèng）：古代四马驾一车为一乘。［6］弑（shì）：下杀上，卑杀尊。［7］苟：如果。［8］餍（yàn）：满足。［9］遗：遗弃。

【译文】孟子谒见梁惠王。梁惠王说："老先生，您不远千里来到这里，一定是有对我的国家有利的高见吧？"

孟子回答说："大王，您何必谈利呢？只讲仁义就行了。大王说：'怎样能对我的国家有利？'大夫说：'怎样能对我的封地有利？'士人和百姓说：'怎样能对我自己有利？'如此上下互相争夺利益，国家就很危险了！在一个拥有一万辆兵车的国家里能够杀害国君的人，一定是拥有一千辆兵车的大夫；在一个拥有一千辆兵车的国家里能够杀害国君的人，一定是拥有一百辆兵车的大夫。这些大夫在一万辆兵车的国家中就拥有一千辆，在一千辆兵车的国家中就拥有一百辆，他们拥有的不可谓不多。可是，如果把义放在后而把利摆在前，他们不夺得国君的地位是永远不会满足的。反之，从来没有讲求仁爱的人而抛弃自己父母的，从来也没有讲求道义而怠慢自己国君的人。所以，大王只讲仁义就行了，何必说利呢？"

　　【解读】孟子所处的战国时代，较春秋时期而言，战乱更加频发，社会动荡加剧，人们竞相逐利，"子弑父、臣弑君"的现象屡屡发生。面对远道而来的孟子，梁惠王首先关注的就是会给自己带来怎样的好处，但孟子举起了不同于世俗的"义旗"，当头棒喝梁惠王，对唯利是图的后果进行了深刻的揭示。孟子认为，如果人们眼中只有利益，必定会致使上下互相争夺利益，那么，整个社会便会因此陷入人人为己的混乱状态。那怎样才能拯救世道人心？孟子响亮地喊出了"亦曰仁义而已矣"，这一口号不仅警醒了当时的社会，而且深刻塑造了后世中华民族的精神世界。当然，义利之辨是儒家所讨论的核心论题，也是当今社会需要我们认真面对的严肃问题。

在本章中孟子所反对的是"后义而先利"，是想让人将"义"放在首要标准。追求名利并不可耻，儒家肯定合乎道义的名利追求，可耻的是在利益面前丧失道德的底线。这也警示我们，切勿陷入一味趋利的泥沼，忘却了道义二字。

1.2

　　孟子见梁惠王，王立于沼 [1] 上，顾鸿雁麋鹿，曰："贤者亦乐此乎？"

　　孟子对曰："贤者而后乐此，不贤者虽有此，不乐也。《诗》云：'经始灵台 [2]，经之营之，庶民攻 [3] 之，不日 [4] 成之。经始勿亟 [5]，庶民子来。王在灵囿 [6]，麀鹿 [7] 攸伏，麀鹿濯濯 [8]，白鸟鹤鹤 [9]。王在灵沼，於牣 [10] 鱼跃。'文王以民力为台为沼。而民欢乐之，谓其台曰'灵台'，谓其沼曰'灵沼'，乐其有麋鹿鱼鳖。古之人与民偕乐，故能乐也。《汤誓》曰：'时日害丧 [11]？予及女 [12] 偕亡。'民欲与之偕亡，虽有台池鸟兽，岂能独乐哉？"

Mencius, another day, saw King Hui of Liang. The king went and stood with him by a pond, and, looking round at the large geese and deer, said, "Do wise and good princes also find pleasure in these things?"

Mencius replied, "Being wise and good, they have pleasure in these things. If they are not wise and good, though they have these things, they do not find pleasure. It is said in the *Book of Poetry*, 'He measured out and commenced his marvellous tower; He measured it out and planned it. The people addressed themselves to it, and in less than a day completed it. When he measured and began it, he said to them — Be not so earnest. But the multitudes came as if they had been his children. The king was in his marvellous park; the does reposed about, the does so sleek and fat; and the white birds came glistening. The king was by his marvellous pond; how full was it of fishes leaping about!' King Wen used the strength of the people to make his tower and his pond, and yet the people rejoiced to do the work, calling the tower 'the marvellous tower', calling the pond 'the marvellous pond', and rejoicing

that he had his large deer, his fishes, and turtles.
The ancients caused the people to have pleasure as
well as themselves, and therefore they could enjoy
it. In the *Declaration of Tang* it is said, 'O sun, when
will you expire? We will die together with you.' The
people wished for Jie's death, though they should
die with him. Although he had towers, ponds, birds,
and animals, how could he have pleasure alone?"

【注释】［1］沼：池塘。［2］经始：开始规划
营建。灵台：故址在今陕西西安。［3］攻：
建造。［4］不日：没几天。［5］亟：同"急"。
［6］灵囿（yòu）：古代帝王畜养禽兽的园林。
［7］麀（yōu）鹿：母鹿。［8］濯（zhuó）濯：
肥胖而光滑的样子。［9］鹤鹤：羽毛洁白的
样子。［10］於（wū）：赞叹词。牣（rèn）：
满。［11］害：同"曷"，即何，意为何时。丧：
毁灭。［12］予及女：我与你。女：同"汝"。

孟子见梁惠王　吴磊　绘

【译文】孟子谒见梁惠王，梁惠王站在池塘旁边，得意地顾盼着鸿雁、麋鹿等飞禽走兽，问孟子说："贤人也以此为乐吗？"

孟子回答说："正因为是贤人才能够以此为乐，不贤的人就算有这些东西，也不能够感到快乐。《诗经》说：'开始规划造灵台，仔细营造巧安排，天下百姓都来干，几天建成速度快。建台本来不着急，百姓似子自动来。大王游览灵园中，母鹿伏在深草丛，母鹿肥大毛色润，白鸟洁净羽毛丰。大王游览到灵沼，满池鱼儿欢跳跃。'周文王动用了民力来修建高台深池。可是百姓都非常高兴，把那台叫作'灵台'，把那池叫作'灵沼'，以那里面有麋鹿鱼鳖等珍禽异兽而快乐。古代的君王与民同乐，所以能真正快乐。相反，《汤誓》说：'你这太阳啊，什么时候毁灭呢？我宁肯与你一起毁灭！'老百姓恨不得与你同归于尽，即使你有高台深池、珍禽异兽，难道能独自享受快乐吗？"

【解读】本章谈论的主旨是怎样才能使自己感到真正的快乐。站在自己的园林中，看鸿雁翱翔、麋鹿腾跃，一片生机盎然，梁惠王情不自禁地问道："贤人也以此为乐吗？"从梁惠王洋洋得意的口气中，完全可以感受到他心中的骄傲自得之情。孟子很坦然，通过周文王与夏桀的民情对比，告诉梁惠王真正的快乐来自与民同乐！作为一国之君，即便是你拥有飞禽走兽而自得其乐，也不是真正的快乐，关键要看你是否得到了百姓的爱戴，这就是贤者"同乐"与不贤者"独乐"的原因。有仁德的君主，应心怀天下苍生，将自己的快乐与百姓共享，如此百姓当然会心甘情愿地拥护他，正如周文王，虽然借用了民力来修建高台深池，可是老百姓都非常高兴。如果将自己的快乐建立在百姓的痛苦之上，如夏桀一般，自诩为太阳，百姓也会诅咒他灭亡，即便与之同归于尽也在所不惜。受人诅咒的人又怎会享受到真正的快乐呢？这实在值得后世为政之人深思。

1.3

梁惠王曰："寡人之于国也，尽心焉耳矣。河内凶，则移其民于河东，移其粟于河内。河东凶亦然。察邻国之政，无如寡人之用心者。邻国之民不加少，寡人之民不加多，何也？"

孟子对曰："王好战，请以战喻。填然鼓之，兵刃既接，弃甲曳兵而走。或百步而后止，或五十步而后止。以五十步笑百步，则何如？"

曰："不可，直[1]不百步耳，是亦走也。"

曰："王如知此，则无望民之多于邻国也。

"不违农时，谷不可胜[2]食也；数罟不入洿池[3]，鱼鳖不可胜食也；斧斤以时入山林，材木不可胜用也。谷与鱼鳖不可胜食，材木不可胜用，是使民养生丧死无憾也。养生丧死无憾，王道之始也。

"五亩之宅，树之以桑，五十者可以衣[4]帛矣；鸡豚狗彘[5]之畜，无失其时，七十者可以食肉矣；百亩之田，勿夺其时，数口之家可以无饥矣；谨庠序之教，申之以孝悌之义，颁白者不负戴于道路矣。七十者衣帛食肉，黎民不饥不寒，然而不王 [6] 者，未之有也。

"狗彘食人食而不知检，涂有饿莩 [7] 而不知发；人死，则曰：'非我也，岁也。'是何异于刺人而杀之，曰：'非我也，兵也。'王无罪岁，斯天下之民至焉。"

King Hui of Liang said, "Small as my virtue is, in the government of my kingdom, I do indeed exert my mind to the utmost. If the year be bad on the inside of the river, I remove as many of the people as I can to the east of the river, and convey grain to the country in the inside. When the year is bad on the east of the river, I act on the same plan. On examining the government of the neighboring kingdoms, I do not find that there is any prince who exerts his mind as I do. And yet the people of the neighboring kingdoms do not decrease, nor do my

孟
子

people increase. How is this?"

Mencius replied, "Your Majesty is fond of war — let me take an illustration from war. The soldiers move forward to the sound of the drums; and after their weapons have been crossed, on one side they throw away their coats of mail, trail their arms behind them, and run. Some run a hundred paces and stop; some run fifty paces and stop. What would you think if those who run fifty paces were to laugh at those who run a hundred paces?"

The king said, "They should not do so. Though they did not run a hundred paces, yet they also ran away."

"Since Your Majesty knows this," replied Mencius.

"you need not hope that your people will become more numerous than those of the neighboring kingdoms. If the seasons of husbandry be not interfered with, the grain will be more than can be eaten. If close nets are not allowed to enter the pools and ponds, the fishes and turtles will be more than can be consumed. If the axes and bills enter the hills and forests only at the proper time, the wood will be more than can be used. When the grain and fish and turtles are more than can be eaten, and there is more wood than can be used, this enables the people to nourish their living and mourn for their dead, without any feeling against any. This condition, in which the people nourish their living and bury their dead without any feeling against any, is the first step of royal government.

Let mulberry trees be planted about the homesteads with their five *mu*, and persons of fifty years may be clothed with silk. In keeping fowls, pigs, dogs, and swine, let not their times of breeding be neglected, and persons of seventy years may eat flesh. Let there not be taken away the time that is proper for the cultivation of the farm with its hundred *mu*, and the family of several mouths that is supported by it shall not suffer from hunger. Let careful attention be paid to education in schools, inculcating in it especially the filial and fraternal duties, and grey-haired men will not be seen upon the roads, carrying burdens on their backs or on their heads. It never has been that the ruler of a state, where such results were seen — persons of seventy wearing silk and eating flesh, and the black-haired people suffering neither from hunger nor cold — did not attain to the royal dignity.

Your dogs and swine eat the food of men, and you do not make any restrictive arrangements. There are people dying from famine on the roads, and you do not issue the stores of your granaries for them. When people die, you say, 'It is not owing to me; it is owing to the year.' In what does this differ from stabbing a man and killing him, and then saying — 'It was not I; it was the weapon?' Let Your Majesty cease to lay the blame on the year, and instantly from all the nation the people will come to you."

【注释】 ［1］直：只是。［2］胜：尽。［3］数罟（cù gǔ）：细密的渔网。数：细密。罟：渔网。洿（wū）池：池塘。［4］衣（yì）：动词，穿。［5］彘（zhì）：猪。［6］王（wàng）：以仁德统一天下。［7］莩（piǎo）：通"殍"，饿死的人。

【译文】 梁惠王说："我对于国家，真的是尽心尽力了。河内遭遇饥荒，就把那里的百姓迁移到河东，把河东的粮食运到河内以赈济；河东遭遇荒年也是如此。观察邻国的政务，没有像我这样用心的。但邻国的百姓并没有减少，我的百姓并没有增多，这是为什么呢？"

孟子回答说："大王您喜欢打仗，请允许我用打仗来比喻。咚咚地击鼓进军，兵器已经相互撞击，有的士兵却扔掉盔甲拖着兵器逃跑。有人跑了一百步停下，有人跑了五十步停下。跑了五十步的人嘲笑跑了一百步的人，这样做怎么样呢？"

梁惠王说："不可以，只不过没有跑到一百步罢了，这也同样是逃跑呀！"

孟子说："大王如果懂得这个道理，那就不必期望您的百姓比邻国多了。

"如果不违背农时，粮食就吃不完；细密的渔网不进池塘捕鱼，鱼鳖就吃不完；按照季节砍伐树木，木材便用不完。粮食和鱼鳖吃不完，木材用不完，这样就使百姓对供养活人埋葬死者没有什么不满。百姓对供养活人埋葬死者都没有不满，这就是王道的开端了。

"五亩大的住宅，里面种上桑树，五十岁的人就可以穿上丝绵衣了；畜养鸡、猪、狗等家禽、家畜，按照它们繁殖的规律去饲养它们，七十岁的人都可以有肉吃了；百亩的耕地，不要耽误种田人的农时，数口人的家庭就不会有挨饿的情况了；认真地兴办学校教育，把孝敬父母、尊重兄长的道理反复讲给百姓听，那么，白发的老人就不会背着东西奔走在道路上了。七十岁的人有丝绵衣穿，有肉吃，普通百姓饿不着、冻不着，这样却不能统一天下的，是不曾有过的事。

"（现在，富贵人家的）猪狗吃掉了人吃的食物却不加制止，路上有饿死的人却不知道打开粮仓赈救灾民。老百姓死了，竟说：'这不是我的罪过，是年成不好造成的。'这种说法和拿着刀子刺死人后，却说：'杀死人的不是我，是兵器'，有什么区别？王不要怪罪于年成不好，这样，天下的百姓都会前来归顺了。"

【解读】在本章中，自我感觉已经用心治国的梁惠王心中充满了委屈：对待自然灾害虽然倾尽全力，结果却仍然是"邻国之民不加少，寡人之民不加多！"不解其中原因，孟子用高超的论辩智慧，解答了梁惠王的疑问。首先，孟子以作战为喻，用"五十步笑百步"的例子，启发梁惠王认识到自己头痛医头，脚痛医脚的做法同其他诸侯并没有本质区别。接着，孟子从根本入手提出了惠民仁政之策。头痛医头、脚痛医脚的小恩小惠是无法真正吸引广大百姓的，要想使百姓归顺，只有施行仁政：首先养民，使百姓"养生丧死无憾"；其次教民，"谨庠序之教，申之以孝悌之义"，让百姓受到教化。如此，才能够从根本上赢得百姓的拥戴。从孟子的描述中，可以感受到孟子"尚和合，求大同"的精神品格，这种精神品格影响了中华民族一代又一代的仁人志士，激励其为了理想的大同社会而奋斗。

此外，孟子在当时能够提出维护生态平衡与自然和谐共生的理念（"数罟不入洿池，鱼鳖不可胜食也；斧斤以时入山林，材木不可胜用也"），也是极为深邃的，反映了古人的生活智慧。

1.4

梁惠王曰："寡人愿安[1]承教。"

孟子对曰："杀人以梃[2]与刃，有以异乎？"

曰："无以异也。"

"以刃与政，有以异乎？"

曰："无以异也。"

曰："庖[3]有肥肉，厩[4]有肥马，民有饥色，野有饿莩，此率兽而食人也。兽相食，且人恶[5]之。为民父母，行政不免于率兽而食人。恶[6]在其为民父母也？仲尼曰：'始作俑[7]者，其无后乎！'为其象[8]人而用之也。如之何其使斯民饥而死也？"

King Hui of Liang said, "I wish quietly to receive your instructions."

Mencius replied, "Is there any difference between killing a man with a stick and with a sword?"

The king said, "There is no difference!"

"Is there any difference between doing it with a sword and with the style of government?"

"There is no difference," was the reply.

Mencius then said, "In your kitchen there is fat meat; in your stables there are fat horses. But your people have the look of hunger, and on the wilds there are those who have died of famine. This is leading on beasts to devour men. Beasts devour one another, and men hate them for doing so. When a prince, being the parent of his people, administers his government so as to be chargeable with leading on beasts to devour men, where is his parental relation to the people? Zhongni said, "Was he not without posterity who first made wooden images to bury with the dead? So he said, because that man made the semblances of men, and used them for that purpose—what shall be thought of him who causes his people to die of hunger?"

【注释】〔1〕安：乐意。〔2〕梃（tǐng）：木棒。〔3〕庖（páo）：厨房。〔4〕厩（jiù）：马棚。〔5〕恶（wù）：讨厌。〔6〕恶（wū）：疑问副词，何，怎么。〔7〕俑：用作陪葬的人形土偶、木偶。〔8〕象：同"像"。

【译文】梁惠王说："我很乐意听您的指教。"

孟子回答说："用木棒打死人和用刀子杀死人，有什么不同吗？"

（梁惠王）说："没有什么不同。"

（孟子又问：）"用刀子杀死人和用苛政害死人，有什么不同吗？"

（梁惠王）回答："没有什么不同。"

（孟子）于是说："厨房里有肥嫩的肉，马棚里有健壮的马，可是老百姓面带饥色，野外躺着饿死的人，这等于是在上位的人率领着野兽吃人啊！野兽自相残杀，人尚且厌恶它。作为老百姓的父母官，施政不能免于率领野兽来吃人，又怎么能够做老百姓的父母官呢？孔子说：'最初采用土偶木偶陪葬的人，该是会断子绝孙吧！'这不过是因为土偶木偶太像活人而用来陪葬罢了。（用俑殉葬尚且不可）又怎么可以使老百姓活活地饿死呢？"

【解读】本章谈论的中心，还是告诫梁惠王，当政者要施仁政于民，关心百姓疾苦。在谈话中，孟子逐步引导梁惠王认识到：作为国君，如果不能够施行仁政，只想使自己"庖有肥肉，厩有肥马"，只追求自己的享乐，而毫不顾及百姓的死活，使百姓"民有饥色，野有饿莩"，陷于涂炭之中，这种苛政行为与用刀棒杀人无异，等同于"率兽而食人"。这种将无道的统治者直斥为禽兽的慷慨之词，可以使我们感受到孟子内心强烈的正义感与傲岸的人格魅力。在孟子心中，统治者并不是被顶礼膜拜的，而是需要教育引导甚至是监督批判的对象。这种犀利睿智的思想，振聋发聩，引人深思。

1.5

梁惠王曰："晋国^[1]，天下莫强焉，叟之所知也。及寡人之身，东败于齐，长子死焉；西丧地于秦七百里；南辱于楚。寡人耻之，愿比死者一洒之^[2]，如之何则可？"

孟子对曰："地方百里而可以王。王如施仁政于民，省刑罚，薄税敛，深耕易耨^[3]，壮者以暇日修其孝悌忠信，入以事其父兄，出以事其长上，可使制梃以挞秦、楚之坚甲利兵矣。

"彼夺其民时，使不得耕耨以养其父母，父母冻饿，兄弟妻子离散。彼陷溺其民，王往而征之，夫谁与王敌？故曰：'仁者无敌。'王请勿疑！"

King Hui of Liang said, "There was not in the nation a stronger state than Jin, as you, venerable sir, know. But since it descended to me, on the

east we have been defeated by Qi, and then my
eldest son perished; on the west we have lost seven
hundred *li* of territory to Qin; and on the south we
have sustained disgrace at the hands of Chu. I have
brought shame on my departed predecessors, and
wish on their account to wipe it away, once for all.
What course is to be pursued to accomplish this?"

Mencius replied, "With a territory which is
only a hundred *li* square, it is possible to attain to the
royal dignity. If Your Majesty will indeed dispense a
benevolent government to the people, being sparing
in the use of punishments and fines, and making
the taxes and levies light, so causing that the fields
shall be ploughed deep, and the weeding of them be
carefully attended to, and that the strong-bodied,
during their days of leisure, shall cultivate their
filial piety, fraternal respectfulness, sincerity, and
truthfulness, serving thereby, at home, their fathers
and elder brothers, and, abroad, their elders and

superiors, —you will then have a people who can be employed, with sticks which they have prepared, to oppose the strong mail and sharp weapons of the troops of Qin and Chu.

The rulers of those states rob their people of their time, so that they cannot plough and weed their fields, in order to support their parents. Their parents suffer from cold and hunger. Brothers, wives, and children are separated and scattered abroad. Those rulers, as it were, drive their people into pitfalls, or drown them. Your Majesty will go to punish them. In such a case, who will oppose Your Majesty? In accordance with this is the saying, 'The benevolent has no enemy.' I beg Your Majesty not to doubt what I say."

【注释】[1]晋国：指魏国。三家分晋而有魏国。[2]比：替，代。一：副词，全，都。洒：洗。[3]易：疾速。耰：一种碎土、平整土地的农具，

29

相当于"耰"（荆条编的整平土地的农具）。
土地耕起后，马上用耰碎土、平整。

【译文】梁惠王说："晋国的强大，当时天下
没有哪个国家能赶得上，这是老先生您知道
的。可是到了我这时候，东边被齐国打败，
连我的大儿子都死了；西边丧失了七百里的
土地给秦国；南边又受楚国的凌辱。我为这
些事感到非常羞耻，希望替所有的死难者报
仇雪恨，我要怎样做才可以呢？"

孟子回答说："只要有方圆一百里的土
地就可以使天下归服。大王如果对老百姓施
行仁政，减免刑罚，少收赋税，深耕细作，
及时平整土地；让身强力壮的人抽出时间修
养孝顺、尊敬、忠诚、守信的品德，在家侍
奉父母兄长，出门尊敬长辈上级，这样就是
让他们制作木棒也可以打击那些拥有坚实盔
甲和锐利刀枪的秦、楚军队了。

"他们（秦国、楚国）的执政者剥夺了

老百姓的生产时间，使百姓不能够靠深耕细作来赡养父母，父母受冻挨饿，兄、弟、妻、子东离西散。他们使老百姓陷入深渊之中，大王去征伐他们，有谁来和您抵抗呢？所以说："施行仁政的人是无敌的。'大王请不要怀疑！"

【解读】本章响亮地提出光耀千古的思想"仁者无敌"。梁惠王对自己所受的耻辱耿耿于怀，所以虚心求教孟子，以求能够洗刷耻辱。孟子则因势利导，使梁惠王认识到，只有施行仁政，教化百姓懂礼法，明是非，心怀仁，使国人皆有正义感；之后再去讨伐暴虐的诸侯国，则无往而不胜，故"仁者无敌"。当然，孟子的这种朴素的仁政思想，带有理想化的色彩，在靠武力征伐来赢得胜利、兼并诸侯的战国时代，甚至显得有些迂腐，却如洪钟大吕般道出了国家强大的真正秘密：民心向背决定了国家的兴衰。只有心想百姓，"省刑罚，薄税敛，深耕易耨"，使百姓过上美好的生活，并且对百姓进行教育，使百姓知礼节，才能得到百姓的拥护，国家才会有自信，这就是"仁者无敌"的力量。真正的力量来自人民的拥护。

1.6

　　孟子见梁襄王。出，语[1]人曰："望之不似人君，就之而不见所畏焉。卒然[2]问曰：'天下恶乎定？'

　　"吾对曰：'定于一。'

　　"'孰能一之？'

　　"对曰：'不嗜杀人者能一之。'

　　"'孰能与[3]之？'

　　"对曰：'天下莫不与也。王知夫苗乎？七八月之间旱，则苗槁矣。天油然作云，沛然下雨，则苗浡然[4]兴之矣。其如是，孰能御之？今夫天下之人牧[5]，未有不嗜杀人者也，如有不嗜杀人者，则天下之民皆引领而望之矣。诚如是也，民归之，由[6]水之就下，沛然谁能御之？'"

Mencius went to see the king Xiang of Liang. On coming out from the interview, he said to some persons, "When I looked at him from a distance, he did not appear like a sovereign; when I drew near to him, I saw nothing venerable about him. Abruptly he asked me, 'How can the kingdom be settled?'

I replied, 'It will be settled by being united under one sway.'

'Who can so unite it?'

I replied, 'He who has no pleasure in killing men can so unite it.'

'Who can give it to him?'

I replied, 'All the people of the nation will unanimously give it to him. Does Your Majesty understand the way of the growing grain? During the seventh and eighth months, when drought prevails, the plants become dry. Then the clouds collect densely in the heavens, they send down torrents of rain, and the grain erects itself, as if by a shoot. When it does so, who can keep it back? Now among the shepherds of men throughout the nation, there is not one who does not find pleasure in killing men. If there were one who did not find pleasure in killing men, all the people in the nation would look towards him with outstretched necks. Such being indeed the case, the people would flock to him, as water flows downwards with a rush, which no one can repress.'"

【注释】［1］语（yù）：动词，告诉。［2］卒然：突然。卒：同"猝"。［3］与：从，跟。［4］浡然：蓬勃地兴起。［5］人牧：治理人民的人，指国君。［6］由：同"犹"，好像。

【译文】孟子拜见了梁襄王。出来后，告诉人说："远看不像个国君，到了他跟前也看不出威严的样子。他突然发问道：'天下要怎样才能安定？'

"我回答说：'要统一才会安定。'

"他又问：'谁能统一天下呢？'

"我回答：'不喜欢杀人的国君能统一

天下。'

"他又问：'有谁愿意跟随不喜欢杀人
的国君呢？'

"我回答：'天下的人没有不喜欢跟随
他的。大王知道禾苗的情况吗？当七八月间
天旱的时候，禾苗就干枯了。一旦天上乌云
密布，哗啦啦下起大雨来，禾苗便会蓬勃生
长起来。这样的情况，谁能够阻挡得了呢？
如今各国的国君，没有一个不喜欢杀人的，
如果有一个不喜欢杀人的国君，那么，天下
的百姓都会伸长脖子期待着他来解救了。真
像这样，老百姓归服他，就像水向低处奔流
一样，奔腾而至谁能阻挡得住呢？"

【解读】本章记述了孟子与梁襄王之间的一次
对话，但这似乎并不是一次愉快的对话，从
谈话中可以看出孟子对梁襄王的评价并不高。
在孟子看来，梁襄王"望之不似人君"，也
没有做君主的威仪。不过，他却与孟子谈论

了一个严肃的问题："天下恶乎定？"从这个问题中，可以看出梁襄王是有称霸天下的野心的。梁襄王是前章中梁惠王的儿子，他继承其父好战的基因，渴望通过战争来建立自己的霸权。

在兼并战争激烈的战国时代，争城以战，杀人盈城；争地以战，杀人盈野。哪个诸侯不是为了自己的霸业而驱使百姓以命相搏呢？哪个诸侯不视百姓如蝼蚁来暴虐百姓呢？而孟子对此深恶痛绝！所以，当梁襄王急切地追问统一天下之道时，孟子回答"不嗜杀人者能一之"，只有爱惜百姓生命的君王才可能统一天下！这既是对当时残暴君主的批判与讽刺，也是对百姓命运的深深同情，老百姓是多么渴望能够遇到仁德的君主，过上安定的生活啊，就像枯萎的禾苗对甘霖的渴望一样！可惜的是，梁襄王并不是仁德的君主，也不能真心接受孟子的这一主张，所以，孟子也在不久后失望地离开了魏国。

1.7

齐宣王问曰："齐桓、晋文之事可得闻乎？"

孟子对曰："仲尼之徒无道桓、文之事者，是以后世无传焉。臣未之闻也。无以 [1]，则王乎？"

曰："德何如，则可以王矣？"

曰："保 [2] 民而王，莫之能御也。"

曰："若寡人者，可以保民乎哉？"

曰："可。"

曰："何由知吾可也？"

曰："臣闻之胡龁 [3] 曰，王坐于堂上，有牵牛而过堂下者，王见之，曰：'牛何之？'对曰：'将以衅钟 [4]。'王曰：'舍之！吾不忍其觳觫 [5]，若无罪而就死地。'对曰：'然则废衅钟与？'曰：'何可废也？以羊易之！'不识有诸？"

曰："有之。"

曰："是心足以王矣。百姓皆以王为爱 [6] 也，臣固知王之不忍也。"

王曰："然。诚有百姓者。齐国虽褊 [7] 小，吾何爱一牛？即不忍其觳觫，若无罪而就死地，故以羊易之也。"

曰："王无异于百姓之以王为爱也。以小易大，彼恶知之？王若隐其无罪而就死地，则牛羊何择焉？"

王笑曰："是诚何心哉？我非爱其财，而易之以羊也，宜乎百姓之谓我爱也。"

曰："无伤也，是乃仁术也，见牛未见羊也。君子之于禽兽也，见其生，不忍见其死；闻其声，不忍食其肉。是以君子远庖厨也。"

王说曰："《诗》云：'他人有心，予忖度 [8] 之。'夫子之谓也。夫我乃行之，反而求之，不得吾心。夫子言之，于我心有戚戚焉。此心之所以合于王者，何也？"

曰："有复于王者曰：'吾力足以举百钧，而不足以举一羽；明足以察秋毫之末，而不见舆薪'，则王许之乎？"

曰："否。"

"今恩足以及禽兽，而功不至于百姓者，独何与？然则一羽之不举，为不用力焉；舆薪之不见，为不用明焉；百姓之不见保，为不用恩焉。故王之不王，不为也，非不能也。"

曰："不为者与不能者之形何以异？"

曰："挟太山以超北海，语人曰'我不能'，是诚不能也。为长者折枝，语人曰'我不能'，是不为也，非不能也。故王之不王，非挟太山以超北海之类也；王之不王，是折枝之类也。老吾老，以及人之老；幼吾幼，以及人之幼。天下可运于掌。《诗》云：'刑[9] 于寡妻[10]，至于兄弟，以御于家邦。'言举斯心加诸彼而已。故推恩足以保四海，不推恩无以保妻子。古之人所以大过人者无他焉，善推其所为而已矣。今恩足以及禽兽，而功不至于百姓者，独何与？权，然后知轻重；度[11]，然后知长短。物皆然，心为甚。王请度之！抑王兴甲兵，危士臣，构怨于诸侯，然后快于心与？"

王曰："否。吾何快于是？将以求吾所大欲也。"

曰："王之所大欲可得闻与？"

王笑而不言。

曰："为肥甘不足于口与？轻暖不足于体与？抑为采色不足视于目与？声音不足听于耳与？便嬖[12]不足使令于前与？王之诸臣皆足以供之，而王岂为是哉？"

曰："否。吾不为是也。"

曰："然则王之所大欲可知已。欲辟土地，朝秦、楚，莅中国而抚四夷也。以若所为，求若所欲，犹缘木而求鱼也。"

王曰："若是其甚与？"

曰："殆有甚焉。缘木求鱼，虽不得鱼，无后灾。以若所为，求若所欲，尽心力而为之，后必有灾。"

曰："可得闻与？"

曰："邹人与楚人战，则王以为孰胜？"

曰："楚人胜。"

曰："然则小固不可以敌大，寡固不可以敌众，弱固不可以敌强。海内之地方千里者九，齐集有其一。以一服八，何以异于邹敌楚哉？盖亦反其本矣。今王发政施仁，使天下仕者皆欲立于王之朝，耕者皆欲耕于王之野，商贾皆欲藏于王之市，行旅皆欲出于王之涂，天下之欲疾其君者皆欲赴愬[13]于王。其若是，孰能御之？"

王曰："吾惛，不能进于是矣。愿夫子辅吾志，明以教我。我虽不敏，请尝试之。"

曰："无恒产而有恒心者，惟士为能。若民，则无恒产，因无恒心。苟无恒心，放辟邪侈，无不为已。及陷于罪，然后从而刑之，是罔[14]民也。焉有仁人在位，罔民而可为也？是故明君制民之产，必使仰足以事父母，俯足以畜妻子；乐岁终身饱，凶年免于死亡。然后驱而之善，故民之从之也轻。今也制民之产，仰不足以事父母，俯不足以畜妻子，乐岁终身苦，凶年不免于死亡。此惟救死而恐不赡^[15]，奚暇治礼义哉？王欲行之，则盍反其本矣。五亩之宅，树之以桑，五十者可以衣帛矣；鸡豚狗彘之畜，无失其时，七十者可以食肉矣；百亩之田，勿夺其时，八口之家可以无饥矣；谨庠序之教，申之以孝悌之义，颁白者不负戴于道路矣。老者衣帛食肉，黎民不饥不寒，然而不王者，未之有也。"

The king Xuan of Qi asked, saying, "May I be informed by you of the transactions of Huan of Qi, and Wen of Jin?"

Mencius replied, "There were none of the disciples of Zhongni who spoke about the affairs of Huan and Wen, and therefore they have not been transmitted to these after ages—your servant has not heard them. If you will have me speak, let it be about royal government."

The king said, "What virtue must there be in

order to attain to royal sway?"

Mencius answered, "The love and protection of the people; with this there is no power which can prevent a ruler from attaining to it."

The king asked again, "Is such a one as I competent to love and protect the people?"

Mencius said, "Yes."

"How do you know that I am competent for that?"

"I heard the following incident from Hu He: —'The king,' said he, 'was sitting aloft in the hall, when a man appeared, leading an ox past the lower part of it. The king saw him, and asked, Where is the ox going? The man replied, We are going to consecrate a bell with its blood. The king said, Let it go. I cannot bear its frightened appearance, as if it were an innocent person going to the place of death. The man answered, Shall we then omit the consecration of the bell? The king said,

How can that be omitted? Change it for a sheep.' I do not know whether this incident really occurred."

The king replied, "It did."

And then Mencius said, "The heart seen in this is sufficient to carry you to the royal sway. The people all supposed that Your Majesty grudged the animal, but your servant knows surely, that it was Your Majesty's not being able to bear the sight, which made you do as you did."

The king said, "You are right. And yet there really was an appearance of what the people condemned. But though Qi be a small and narrow state, how should I grudge one ox? Indeed it was because I could not bear its frightened appearance, as if it were an innocent person going to the place of death, that therefore I changed it for a sheep."

Mencius pursued, "Let not Your Majesty deem it strange that the people should think you were grudging the animal. When you changed a large one for a small, how should they know the true reason? If you felt pained by its being led without guilt to the place of death, what was there to choose between an ox and a sheep?"

The king laughed and said, "What really was my mind in the matter? I did not grudge the expense of it, and changed it for a sheep! There was reason in the people's saying that I grudged it."

"There is no harm in their saying so," said Mencius. "Your conduct was an artifice of benevolence. You saw the ox, and had not seen the sheep. So is the superior man affected towards animals, that, having seen them alive, he cannot bear to see them die; having heard their dying cries, he cannot bear to eat their flesh. Therefore he keeps away from his slaughterhouse and cook-room."

The king was pleased, and said, "It is said in the *Book of Poetry*, 'The minds of others, I am able by reflection to measure;' — this is verified, my

Master, in your discovery of my motive. I indeed did the thing, but when I turned my thoughts inward, and examined into it, I could not discover my own mind. When you, Master, spoke those words, the movements of compassion began to work in my mind. How is it that this heart has in it what is equal to the royal sway?"

Mencius replied, "Suppose a man were to make this statement to Your Majesty, 'My strength is sufficient to lift three thousand catties, but it is not sufficient to lift one feather; my eyesight is sharp enough to examine the point of an autumn hair, but I do not see a waggon-load of faggots.' Would Your Majesty allow what he said?"

"No," was the answer, on which Mencius proceeded.

"Now here is kindness sufficient to reach to animals, and no benefits are extended from it to the people. —How is this? Is an exception to be made

孟
子

here? The truth is, the feather is not lifted, because

strength is not used; the waggon-load of firewood

is not seen, because the eyesight is not used; and

the people are not loved and protected, because

kindness is not employed. Therefore Your Majesty's

not exercising the royal sway, is because you do not

do it, not because you are not able to do it."

The king asked, "How may the difference

between the not doing a thing, and the not being

able to do it, be represented?"

Mencius replied, "In such a thing as taking

the Tai mountain under your arm, and leaping over

the north sea with it, if you say to people 'I am not

able to do it,' that is a real case of not being able. In

such a matter as breaking off a branch from a tree

at the order of a superior, if you say to people— 'I

am not able to do it,' that is a case of not doing it,

it is not a case of not being able to do it. Therefore

Your Majesty's not exercising the royal sway, is not

such a case as that of taking the Tai mountain under your arm, and leaping over the north sea with it. Your Majesty's not exercising the royal sway is a case like that of breaking off a branch from a tree. Treat with the reverence due to age the elders in your own family, so that the elders in the families of others shall be similarly treated; treat with the kindness due to youth the young in your own family, so that the young in the families of others shall be similarly treated—do this, and the kingdom may be made to go round in your palm. It is said in the *Book of Poetry*, 'His example affected his wife. It reached to his brothers, and his family of the State was governed by it.' The language shows how king Wen simply took his kindly heart, and exercised it towards those parties. Therefore the carrying out his kindness of heart by a prince will suffice for the love and protection of all within the four seas, and if he do not carry it out, he will not be able to protect his wife and children. The way in which the ancients came greatly to surpass other men, was no other but this—simply that they knew well how to carry out, so as to affect others, what they themselves did. Now your kindness is sufficient to reach to animals, and no benefits are extended from it to reach the people. How is this? Is an exception to be made here? By weighing, we know what things are light, and what heavy. By measuring, we know what things are long, and what short. The relations of all things may be thus determined, and it is of the greatest importance to estimate the motions of the mind. I beg Your Majesty to measure it. You collect your equipments of war, endanger your soldiers and officers, and excite the resentment of the other princes—do these things cause you pleasure in your mind?"

The king replied, "No. How should I derive pleasure from these things? My object in them is to seek for what I greatly desire."

Mencius said, "May I hear from you what it is that you greatly desire?"

The king laughed and did not speak.

Mencius resumed, "Are you led to desire it, because you have not enough of rich and sweet food for your mouth? Or because you have not enough of light and warm clothing for your body? Or because you have not enough of beautifully coloured objects to delight your eyes? Or because you have not voices and tones enough to please your ears? Or because you have not enough of attendants and favourites to stand before you and receive your orders? Your Majesty's various officers are sufficient to supply you with those things. How can Your Majesty be led to entertain such a desire on account of them?"

"No," said the king, "my desire is not on account of them."

Mencius added, "Then, what Your Majesty greatly desires may be known. You wish to enlarge your territories, to have Qin and Chu wait at your court, to rule the Middle Kingdom, and to attract to you the barbarous tribes that surround it. But doing what you do to seek for what you desire is like climbing a tree to seek for fish."

The king said, "Is it so bad as that?"

"It is even worse," was the reply. "If you climb a tree to seek for fish, although you do not get the fish, you will not suffer any subsequent calamity. But doing what you do to seek for what you desire, doing it moreover with all your heart, you will assuredly afterwards meet with calamities."

The king asked, "May I hear from you the proof of that?"

Mencius said, "If the people of Zou should fight with the people of Chu, which of them does Your Majesty think would conquer?"

"The people of Chu would conquer."

"Yes; —and so it is certain that a small country

cannot contend with a great, that few cannot contend with many, that the weak cannot contend with the strong. The territory within the four seas embraces nine divisions, each of a thousand *li* square. All Qi together is but one of them. If with one part you try to subdue the other eight, what is the difference between that and Zou's contending with Chu? For, with such a desire, you must turn back to the proper course for its attainment. Now if Your Majesty will institute a government whose action shall be benevolent, this will cause all the officers in the kingdom to wish to stand in Your Majesty's court, and all the farmers to wish to plough in Your Majesty's fields, and all the merchants, both travelling and stationary, to wish to store their goods in Your Majesty's marketplaces, and all travelling strangers to wish to make their tours on Your Majesty's roads, and all throughout the kingdom who feel aggrieved by their rulers to wish to come and complain to Your Majesty. And when they are so bent, who will be able to keep them back?"

The king said, "I am stupid, and not able to advance to this. I wish you, my Master, to assist my intentions. Teach me clearly; although I am deficient in intelligence and vigour, I will essay and try to carry your instructions into effect."

Mencius replied, "They are only men of education, who, without a certain livelihood, are able to maintain a fixed heart. As to the people, if they have not a certain livelihood, it follows that they will not have a fixed heart. And if they have not a fixed heart, there is nothing which they will not do, in the way of self-abandonment, of moral deflection, of depravity, and of wild license. When they thus have been involved in crime, to follow them up and punish them; —this is to entrap the people. How can such a thing as entrapping the people be done under the rule of a benevolent man? Therefore an intelligent ruler will regulate the livelihood of the people, so as to make sure that, for those above them, they shall have sufficient wherewith to serve their parents, and, for those below them, sufficient wherewith to support their wives and children; that in good years they shall always be abundantly satisfied, and that in bad years they shall escape the danger of perishing. After this he may urge them, and they will proceed to what is good, for in this case the people will follow after it with ease. Now, the livelihood of the people is so regulated, that, above, they have not sufficient wherewith to serve their parents, and, below, they have not sufficient wherewith to support their wives and children. Notwithstanding good years, their lives are continually embittered, and, in bad years, they do not escape perishing. In such circumstances they only try to save themselves from death, and are afraid they will not succeed. What leisure have they to cultivate propriety and righteousness? If

Your Majesty wishes to effect this regulation of the livelihood of the people, why not turn to that which is the essential step to it? Let mulberry trees be planted about the homesteads with their five *mu*, and persons of fifty years may be clothed with silk. In keeping fowls, pigs, dogs, and swine, let not their times of breeding be neglected, and persons of seventy years may eat flesh. Let there not be taken away the time that is proper for the cultivation of the farm with its hundred *mu*, and the family of eight mouths that is supported by it shall not suffer from hunger. Let careful attention be paid to education in schools, —the inculcation in it especially of the filial and fraternal duties, and grey-haired men will not be seen upon the roads, carrying burdens on their backs or on their heads. It never has been that the ruler of a state where such results were seen, — the old wearing silk and eating flesh, and the black-haired people suffering neither from hunger nor cold, did not attain to the royal dignity."

【注释】［1］无以：不得已。［2］保：安。［3］
胡龁（hé）：齐宣王的近臣。［4］衅钟：杀
牲以血涂钟行祭。［5］觳觫（hú sù）：因恐
惧而发抖。［6］爱：吝啬，吝惜。［7］褊（biǎn）：
狭小。［8］忖度（cǔn duó）：推测，揣度。
［9］刑：通"型"，示范。［10］寡妻：嫡
妻。［11］度（duó）：动词，用尺子量。［12］
便嬖（pián bì）：能说会道、善于迎合的宠幸
者。［13］愬（sù）：同"诉"，诉说，告发。
［14］罔：欺骗，陷害。［15］赡：足够。

【译文】齐宣王问孟子说："齐桓公、晋文公
称霸的事情可以讲给我听吗？"

孟子说："孔子的弟子没有谈论齐桓公、
晋文公之事，因此后世失传了。我没有听说
过这事。如果非要说的话，那么我还是说说
行王道的事？"

（齐宣王）说："要有什么样的德行，才可以称王于天下呢？"

（孟子）说："使民安定来称王，没有人可以抵御得了他。"

（齐宣王）说："像我这样的人，能够使百姓安定吗？"

（孟子）说："可以。"

（齐宣王）说："您根据什么说我可以呢？"

（孟子）说："我从胡龁那里听说，（有一次）您坐在大殿上，有个人牵牛从堂下走过，您看见了，问道：'这牛牵到哪里去？'那人回答说：'准备杀了，用它来祭钟。'您说：'放了它！我不忍看到它那恐惧战栗的样子，就好像（一个人）没有罪却把他置于死地。'那人问道：'既然这样，要废除祭钟的仪式吗？'您说：'怎么可以废除呢？用羊来替换它吧。'不知道有没有这件事？"

（齐宣王）说："有这事。"

（孟子）说：“有这样的仁慈之心就足以称王于天下了。百姓都认为大王这种行为是出于吝啬，而我知道您是于心不忍。”

齐宣王说：“是的。的确有这样误解我的百姓。齐国的土地虽然狭小，我何至于吝惜一头牛？我就是不忍看它那恐惧战栗的样子，就像（一个人）无罪却将它置于死地，因此用羊去替换它。”

（孟子）说：“您不要责怪百姓认为您吝啬。以小换大，他们怎么理解您的想法呢？您如果吝惜它无罪却将其置于死地，那么牛和羊又有什么区别呢？”

齐宣王笑着说：“这究竟是出于什么心理呢？我的确不是吝惜钱财，但以羊替换牛，也难怪老百姓说我吝啬了。”

（孟子）说：“没有关系，这是体现了仁爱之道，只是您看到了牛发抖而没看到羊发抖。有道德的人对于飞禽走兽，看见它活着，便不忍心看它死；听到它哀鸣的声音，便不忍心吃它的肉。因此君子远离宰杀的厨房。"

齐宣王高兴地说："《诗经》说：'别人有什么心思，我能揣测到。'说的就是先生您这样的人啊。我这样做了，回头再去想它，却想不出是为什么。先生您说的这些，对于我的心真是有所触动啊。这种心思之所以符合王道，是为什么呢？"

（孟子）说："假如有人报告大王说：'我的力气足以举起三千斤的重物，而他却不能够举起一根羽毛；我的眼力足以看清鸟兽秋天新生细毛的末梢，而他却看不到整车的柴草。'那么，大王您相信吗？"

（齐宣王）说："不相信。"

（孟子说：）"如今您的恩德足以施及禽兽，而老百姓却得不到您的恩泽，这是为什么呢？如此举不起一根羽毛，是不用力气的缘故；看不见整车的柴草，是不用目力的缘故；百姓没有感受到您的爱护，是您不肯布施恩德的缘故。所以，大王您不能以王道统一天下，是不肯这么做，而不是不能做。"

（齐宣王）说："不肯做与不能做，在表现上怎样区别？"

（孟子）说："用胳臂挟着泰山跳过渤海，告诉别人说：'我做不到。'这确实是做不到。为长辈按摩肢身，告诉别人说：'我做不到。'这是不肯做，而不是不能做。所以大王不能统一天下，不属于用胳臂挟泰山跳过渤海这一类的事；大王不能统一天下，是属于为长辈按摩肢身一类的事。尊敬自己的老人，进而推广到尊敬别人家的老人；爱护自己的孩子，进而推广到爱护别人家的孩子。照此理去做，要统一天下就如同在手掌上转动东西那么容易。《诗经》说：'先做好榜样给自己的妻子看，然后推及兄弟，进而治理好一家一国。'说的就是把这样的心思推广到他人罢了。所以，推广恩德足以安抚四海百姓，不推广恩德连妻子儿女也安抚不了。古代圣人大大超过别人的原因没别的，善于推广他

们的好行为罢了。如今您的恩德足以推广到
禽兽身上，可是功德却不能惠及百姓，这究
竟是什么原因呢？权衡一下，才能知道轻重；
丈量一下，才能知道长短。事物都是如此，
人心更是这样。大王，您请思量一下吧！您
发动战争，危及将士的生命，与各诸侯国结怨，
这样心里才痛快吗？"

（齐宣王）说："不是的。我怎么会对
这种情况感到痛快呢？我是打算用这办法求
得我最想要的东西罢了。"

（孟子）说："您最想要的东西是什么，
可以说给我听听吗？"

齐宣王笑而不语。

（孟子）说："是因为肥美甘甜的食物
不够吃呢？又轻又暖的衣服不够穿呢？还是
因为各种色彩不够看呢？美妙的音乐不够听
呢？左右受宠爱的人不够用呢？这些您的大
臣们都能充分地供给，难道大王真是为了这
些吗？"

（齐宣王）说："不是。我不是为了这些。"

（孟子）说："这样说来，大王所最想得到的东西便可知道了，是想开拓疆土，使秦国、楚国来朝见，统治整个中原地区而安抚四方的民族。但是以您的做法去谋求这样的理想，就像爬到树上去抓鱼一样。"

（齐宣王）说："有像你说的这么严重吗？"

（孟子）说："恐怕比这还严重。爬到树上去抓鱼，虽然抓不到鱼，却没有什么后祸。假使用您的做法，去谋求这样的理想，又尽心尽力地去干，结果必然有灾祸。"

（齐宣王）说："是什么道理，可以讲给我听吗？"

（孟子）说："如果邹国和楚国交战，那您认为谁胜呢？"

（齐宣王）说："楚国会胜。"

（孟子）说："如此说来，小国本来就敌不过大国，兵力少的本来就敌不过兵力多的，弱国本来就敌不过强国。天下的土地，纵横各一千里的国家有九份，齐国的土地全部加起来也只占其中的一份。以一去降服八，这与邹国和楚国为敌有什么不同呢？还是回到根本上来吧。如果您现在发布政令施行仁政，使得天下为官的都想到您的朝廷来做官，种田的都想到您的田野来耕作，做生意的都想把货物存放在大王的集市上，出行的人都想在大王的道路上出入，各国那些憎恨他们君主的人都想跑来向您申诉。如果像这样，谁还能抵挡您呢？"

（齐宣王）说："我糊涂，不能懂得这个道理。希望先生您帮助我实现我的愿望，明确地指导我。我虽然不聪慧，却愿意试着去做。"

（孟子）说："没有长期赖以为生的产业而有恒心的，只有有志之士才能做到。至于百姓，如果没有固定的产业，就没有长久不变的心。如果没有长久不变的心，就会放肆不拘，胡作非为。等到他们犯了罪，随后才用刑法去处罚他们，这样做是陷害百姓。哪有仁爱的君主掌权，却做出这种陷害百姓的事呢？所以贤明的君主规划老百姓的产业，一定使他们上能赡养父母，下能养活妻子儿女；年成好时能丰衣足食，年成不好也不致饿死。然后再督促他们向善，这样老百姓追随国君就容易了。如今规划给百姓的产业，上不能赡养父母，下不能养活妻子儿女；好年景也总是生活在困苦之中，坏年景免不了要饿死。这（就使百姓）连救死济亡还怕来不及，哪里还顾得上学习礼义呢？大王真想施行仁政，应该回到根本上来啊。每家五亩地的住宅，种上桑树，那么五十岁的人就可以穿上丝绵衣了；鸡、猪、狗这些家畜，不扰乱喂养繁殖的时节，七十岁的人就可以有肉吃了；一百亩的田地，不要因劳役耽误了农时，八口人的家庭就可以不挨饿了；重视乡里学校教育，反复地教导他们孝顺父母、

尊重兄长的道理，头发斑白的老人便不会再
背着东西在路上奔走了。老年人都可以穿丝
绵衣、有肉吃，百姓不挨饿受冻，如果像这
样还不能统一天下的，那是没有的事。"

【解读】本章为《孟子》中篇幅最长的一章，
同时也是展现孟子"仁政"主张最为透彻的
一章。齐宣王怀称雄争霸之心，故开始便询
问孟子齐桓公与晋文公的事迹。按照孟子自
身的学识水平来讲，他应当是通晓的，然而
儒家思想的传统是反对以武力、霸道征服天
下。据《论语》记载，卫灵公曾问军阵之事
于孔子，孔子回答说："俎豆之事则尝闻之矣，
军旅之事未之学也。"（《论语·卫灵公》）
故孟子言不知齐桓、晋文之事，非不知也，
实不答也。然而孟子此时抓住了齐宣王的称
霸心理，先将话题引入"王道"之上，称"保
民"即可为王；随后，又为齐宣王以羊易牛
之事正名，并赞扬其有达到"王道"的基础，

坐而论道　岳海波　绘

即"不忍"之心，这无疑让齐宣王感到欣喜。但孟子绝不是谄媚之人，在齐宣王高兴之际，采用归谬法，让齐宣王认识到自己之所以"不王"，是因为"不为"；同时又通过邹楚之战的假设，让齐宣王认识到自己行为的不可行性与危险性。有了以上的前提，孟子才提出了自己的政治蓝图：先令民众有"恒产"，然后在此基础上行教化（这也继承了孔子"庶之""富之""教之"的思想）。这个政治蓝图极为具体翔实，又有可操作性，既保障了民众的生活，又保障了统治政权的稳固，可以说是实现了两个群体的利益最大化。虽然孟子的这一政治蓝图没能在当时实现，却深刻影响了中华民族的文化心理，激励着中华民族一代又一代仁人志士"为万世开太平"。

梁惠王下

2.1

庄暴[1]见孟子，曰："暴见于王[2]，王语暴以好乐，暴未有以对也。"曰："好乐何如？"

孟子曰："王之好乐甚，则齐国其庶几[3]乎！"

他日，见于王，曰："王尝语庄子以好乐，有诸？"

王变乎色，曰："寡人非能好先王之乐也，直好世俗之乐耳。"

曰："王之好乐甚，则齐其庶几乎！今之乐犹古之乐也。"

曰："可得闻与？"

曰："独乐乐[4]，与人乐乐，孰乐？"

曰："不若与人。"

曰："与少乐乐，与众乐乐，孰乐？"

曰："不若与众。"

"臣请为王言乐：今王鼓乐于此，百姓

闻王钟鼓之声，管籥[5]之音，举[6]疾首蹙頞
而相告曰：'吾王之好鼓乐，夫何使我至于
此极[7]也？父子不相见，兄弟妻子离散。'
今王田猎于此，百姓闻王车马之音，见羽旄[8]
之美，举疾首蹙頞而相告曰：'吾王之好田猎，
夫何使我至于此极也？父子不相见，兄弟妻
子离散。'此无他，不与民同乐也。

　　"今王鼓乐于此，百姓闻王钟鼓之声，
管籥之音，举欣欣然有喜色而相告曰：'吾
王庶几无疾病与，何以能鼓乐也？'今王田
猎于此，百姓闻王车马之音，见羽旄之美，
举欣欣然有喜色而相告曰：'吾王庶几无疾
病与，何以能田猎也？'此无他，与民同乐也。
今王与百姓同乐，则王矣。"

Zhuang Bao, seeing Mencius, said to him, "I
had an interview with the king. His Majesty told me
that he loved music, and I was not prepared with
anything to reply to him. What do you pronounce

about that love of music?"

Mencius replied, "If the king's love of music were very great, the kingdom of Qi would be near to a state of good government!"

Another day, Mencius, having an interview with the king, said, "Your Majesty, I have heard, told the officer Zhuang, that you love music, —was it so?"

The king changed colour, and said, "I am unable to love the music of the ancient sovereigns; I only love the music that suits the manners of the present age."

Mencius said, "If Your Majesty's love of music were very great, Qi would be near to a state of good government! The music of the present day is just like the music of antiquity, as regards effecting that."

The king said, "May I hear from you the proof of that?"

Mencius asked, "Which is the more pleasant,

—to enjoy music by yourself alone, or to enjoy it with others?"

"To enjoy it with others," was the reply.

"And which is the more pleasant—to enjoy music with a few, or to enjoy it with many?"

"To enjoy it with many."

Mencius proceeded, "Your servant begs to explain what I have said about music to Your Majesty. Now, Your Majesty is having music here. The people hear the noise of your bells and drums, and the notes of your fifes and pipes, and they all, with aching heads, knit their brows, and say to one another, 'That's how our king likes his music! But why does he reduce us to this extremity of distress? Fathers and sons cannot see one another. Elder brothers and younger brothers, wives and children, are separated and scattered abroad.' Now, Your Majesty is hunting here. The people hear the noise of your carriages and horses, and see the beauty of your plumes and streamers, and they all, with aching heads, knit their brows, and say to one another, 'That's how our king likes his hunting! But why does he reduce us to this extremity of distress? Fathers and sons cannot see one another. Elder brothers and younger brothers, wives and children, are separated and scattered abroad.' Their feeling thus is from no other reason but that you do not allow the people to have pleasure as well as yourself.

Now, Your Majesty is having music here. The people hear the noise of your bells and drums, and the notes of your fifes and pipes, and they all, delighted, and with joyful looks, say to one another, 'That sounds as if our king were free from all sickness! If he were not, how could he enjoy this music?' Now, Your Majesty is hunting here. The people hear the noise of your carriages and horses, and see the beauty of your plumes and streamers, and they all, delighted, and with joyful looks, say to one another, 'That looks as if our king were free from all sickness! If he were not, how could he enjoy this hunting?' Their feeling thus is from no other reason but that you cause them to have their pleasure as you have yours. If Your Majesty now will make pleasure a thing common to the people and yourself, the royal sway awaits you."

【注释】[1]庄暴：齐国大夫。[2]王：指齐宣王。[3]庶几：近，差不多。[4]乐乐（yuè lè）：第一个"乐"是音乐，名词用作动词，指欣赏音乐；第二个"乐"是快乐。[5]管籥（yuè）：古代吹奏乐器。[6]举：都，全。蹙頞（cù è）：皱着眉头。頞：鼻梁，也同"额"。[7]极：穷。[8]羽旄（máo）：用羽毛、牦牛尾装饰的旗子。

【译文】庄暴来见孟子，说："我被召去见大王，王告诉我他喜好音乐的事，我不知道应该如何回答。”又接着说道：“喜好音乐是好还是不好呢？”

孟子说：“大王如果非常喜好音乐，那齐国就差不多治理好了！”

几天后，孟子在觐见齐宣王时问道：“大王曾经和庄暴谈论过您爱好音乐，有这回事吗？”

齐宣王脸色一变，说：“我并不是喜好古代的音乐，我只不过是喜好世俗的音乐罢了。”

（孟子）说：“如果大王您非常喜好音乐，那齐国恐怕就治理得差不多了！在这件事上，现在的俗乐与古代的雅乐差不多。”

（齐宣王）说：“能让我知道是什么道理吗？”

（孟子）说：“独自一人欣赏音乐的快乐，和与他人一起欣赏音乐的快乐，哪个感觉更快乐？”

（齐宣王）说：“不如与他人一起欣赏

音乐更快乐。"

（孟子）说："与少数人欣赏音乐的快乐，
和多数人一起欣赏音乐的快乐，哪个感觉更
快乐？"

（齐宣王）说："不如与多数人一起欣
赏音乐更快乐。"

（孟子说：）"请让我给大王讲讲什么是
真正的快乐吧！假如大王在奏乐，百姓们听
到大王鸣钟击鼓、吹箫奏笛的声音，都愁眉
苦脸地奔走相告说：'我们大王喜好音乐，
为什么却使我们这般穷困呢？父子不能相见，
兄弟妻儿分离流散。'假如大王在围猎，百
姓们听到大王车马的喧嚣，见到华丽的旌旗，
都愁眉苦脸地奔走相告说：'我们大王喜好
围猎，为什么却使我们这般穷困呢？父子不
能相见，兄弟妻儿分离流散。'为什么会有
这种不良影响呢？这没有别的原因，是由于
不和民众同乐的缘故。

"假如大王在奏乐，百姓们听到大王鸣

钟击鼓、吹箫奏笛的声音，都眉开眼笑地奔走相告说：'我们大王大概身体没有什么疾病吧？要不怎么能奏乐呢？'假如大王在围猎，百姓们听到大王车马的喧嚣，见到华丽的旌旗，都眉开眼笑地奔走相告说：'我们大王大概身体没有什么疾病吧？要不怎么能打猎呢？'为什么又会产生这种良好影响呢？这没有别的原因，是由于和民众同乐的缘故。假如大王能和百姓们同乐，那就可以成就王道了。"

【解读】孟子在本章中阐发的是"与民同乐"的政治主张，从"独乐乐"和"与人乐乐"两个方面来论述其产生的两种不同的结果，体现的是他的"仁政"理想和民本思想。

本章的话题是从音乐谈起，儒家思想体系里"乐"与"礼"密切相关，"礼乐"是中国传统文化的重要元素，它与治国理政息息相关，如《礼记·乐记》中所言："治世之音安以乐，其政和；乱世之音怨以怒，其政乖；亡国之音哀以思，其民困。声音之道，与政通矣。"阐述了声音之道与政通、音乐与政治相关联，可见古圣先贤非常重视礼乐的教化作用和治世功能。显然孟子的目的并不是阐发欣赏什么音乐的道理，而是借题发挥，逐步把齐宣王的思路引进自己预设的轨迹。所以，孟子在这里借助欣赏音乐与田猎而剖析阐发治国之道，把抽象的道理形象化，把深奥的乐理具象化，使得"与民同乐"和"不与民同乐"的利弊变得显而易见。朱熹说："与民同乐者，推好乐之心以行仁政，使民各得其所也。""好乐而能与百姓同之，则天下之民归之矣，所谓齐其庶几者如此。"（朱熹《四书章句集注》）朱熹之语可谓切中肯綮，如果一国之君对百姓处于水深火热之中视而不见，使父子兄弟不相见，妻子儿女离散，百姓生活永无宁日，那么，百姓是不会为君王效命的。这样，国家就危险了。

2.2

齐宣王问曰：“文王之囿 [1] 方七十里，有诸？”

孟子对曰：“于传 [2] 有之。”

曰：“若是其大乎？”

曰：“民犹以为小也。”

曰：“寡人之囿方四十里，民犹以为大，何也？”

曰：“文王之囿方七十里，刍荛 [3] 者往焉，雉兔者往焉，与民同之。民以为小，不亦宜乎？臣始至于境，问国之大禁，然后敢入。臣闻郊关之内有囿方四十里，杀其麋鹿者，如杀人之罪，则是方四十里为阱于国中。民以为大，不亦宜乎？”

The king Xuan of Qi asked, "Was it so, that the park of king Wen contained seventy square *li*?"

Mencius replied, "It is so in the records."

"Was it so large as that?" exclaimed the king.

"The people," said Mencius, "still looked on it as small."

The king added, "My park contains only forty square *li*, and the people still look on it as large. How is this?"

"The park of king Wen," was the reply, "contained seventy square *li*, but the grass-cutters and fuel-gatherers had the privilege of entrance into it; so also had the catchers of pheasants and hares. He shared it with the people, and was it not with reason that they looked on it as small? When I first arrived at the borders of your kingdom, I inquired about the great prohibitory regulations, before I would venture to enter it; and I heard, that inside the barrier-gates there was a park of forty square *li*, and that he who killed a deer in it, was held guilty of the same crime as if he had killed a man. Thus those forty square *li* are a pitfall in the middle of the kingdom. Is it not with reason that the people look upon them as *large?"*

【注释】［1］囿：园林，猎场。［2］传：书传，著作。［3］刍荛（chú ráo）：割草打柴。

【译文】齐宣王问道："文王的园林方圆七十里，有这回事吗？"

孟子答道："在文献上有记载。"

（齐宣王）说："像这样是不是大了点？"

（孟子）说："百姓还是以为太小了。"

（齐宣王）说："我的园林方圆才四十里，百姓都以为太大，这是为什么呢？"

（孟子）说："文王的园林方圆七十里，割草砍柴的人去那里，捕鸟打兔子的人也去那里，与百姓共享。因此，百姓以为太小，不也是应该的吗？我刚到齐国的边境时，先打听国家的重要禁令，然后才敢进入。我听说齐国城郊有园林方圆四十里，如果有人杀掉里面的麋鹿，就同杀人一样治罪。那么这方圆四十里就是一个园内的大陷阱，百姓以为太大了，这不也是有道理的吗？"

【解读】本章论述的主题是"与民共享"，其本质还是"仁政"思想。话题是围绕着君王的园囿展开的，园囿是古时君王田猎之所，齐宣王困惑不解的是，为什么百姓抱怨他的园囿面积大而认为周文王的园囿小呢？周文王是被孔子尊奉为圣贤的古圣先王，孟子旗帜鲜明地主张"法先王"，极力推崇文王。孟子的解答可谓直截了当，通过两者的对比，一个"与民同之"，一个"阱于国中"，解答了齐宣王心中的迷惑。在这一大一小的对比中，孟子强调"与民同享"的仁政思想。朱熹曰："囿者，蓄育鸟兽之所。古者四时之田，皆于农隙以讲武事，然不欲驰骛于稼穑场圃之中，故度闲旷之地以为囿。然文王七十里之囿，其亦三分天下有其二之后也

齐宣王田猎园囿图　杨文森　绘

与？"（朱熹《四书章句集注》）园囿的大小不是问题的关键，问题的关键是能否与百姓共享之，不能与民共享，百姓就会背弃你。只有与民同乐同享，才能深得民心，得到民众的拥护。

2.3

齐宣王问曰："交邻国有道乎？"

孟子对曰："有。惟仁者为能以大事小，是故汤事葛[1]，文王事昆夷[2]；惟智者为能以小事大，故大王事獯鬻[3]，句践事吴[4]。以大事小者，乐天者也；以小事大者，畏天者也。乐天者保天下，畏天者保其国。《诗》云：'畏天之威，于时保之。'"

王曰："大哉言矣！寡人有疾，寡人好勇。"

对曰："王请无好小勇。夫抚剑疾视，曰：'彼恶敢当我哉！'此匹夫之勇，敌一人者也。王请大之！《诗》云：'王赫斯[5]怒，爰[6]整其旅，以遏徂莒[7]，以笃周祜[8]，以对于天下。'此文王之勇也。文王一怒而安天下之民。《书》曰：'天降下民，作之君，作之师。惟曰其助上帝，宠之四方。有罪无罪，惟我在，天下曷敢有越厥[9]志？'一人衡行[10]于天下，武王耻之。此武王之勇也。而武王亦一怒而安

天下之民。今 [11] 王亦一怒而安天下之民，民
惟恐王之不好勇也。"

The king Xuan of Qi asked, saying, "Is there
any way to regulate one's maintenance of intercourse
with neighbouring kingdoms?"

Mencius replied, "There is. But it requires a
perfectly virtuous prince to be able, with a great
country, to serve a small one, —as, for instance,
Tang served Ge, and king Wen served the Kun
barbarians. And it requires a wise prince to be
able, with a small country, to serve a large one—
as the king Tai served the Xun Yu, and Gou Jian
served Wu. He who with a great state serves a small
one, delights in Heaven. He who with a small state
serves a large one, stands in awe of Heaven. He
who delights in Heaven, will affect with his love
and protection the whole kingdom. He who stands
in awe of Heaven, will affect with his love and

protection his own kingdom. It is said in the *Book of Poetry*, "I fear the Majesty of Heaven, and will thus preserve its favouring decree.'"

The king said, "A great saying! But I have an infirmity, —I love valour."

"I beg Your Majesty," was the reply, "not to love small valour. If a man brandishes his sword, looks fiercely, and says, 'How dare he withstand me?' —this is the valour of a common man, who can be the opponent only of a single individual. I beg Your Majesty to greaten it. It is said in the *Book of Poetry*, 'The king blazed with anger, and he marshalled his hosts, to stop the march to Chu, to consolidate the prosperity of Zhou, to meet the expectations of the nation.' This was the valour of king Wen. King Wen, in one burst of his anger, gave repose to all the people of the kingdom. In the *Book of History* it is said, 'Heaven having produced the inferior people, made for them rulers and teachers, with the purpose that they should be assisting to God, and therefore distinguished them throughout the four quarters of the land. Whoever are offenders, and whoever are innocent, here am I to deal with them. How dare any under Heaven give indulgence to their refractory wills?' There was one man pursuing a violent and disorderly course in the kingdom, and king Wu was ashamed of it. This was the valour of king Wu. He also, by one display of his anger, gave repose to all the people of the kingdom. Let now Your Majesty also, in one burst of anger, give repose to all the people of the kingdom. The people are only afraid that Your Majesty does not love valour."

【注释】［1］葛：葛伯，葛国的国君。葛国是紧邻商的小国，故城在今河南宁陵北十五里处。［2］昆夷，也写作"混夷"，周朝初年的西戎国名。［3］大王：即周太王古公亶父，文王的祖父。獯鬻（xūn yù）：即猃狁（xiǎn yǔn），古代北方少数民族。〔4〕句践事吴：越王句践被吴王夫差打败屈服求和，以臣事吴。后卧薪尝胆，灭吴。〔5〕赫斯：勃然发怒的样子。〔6〕爰（yuán）：于是。〔7〕遏：止。徂：往，到。莒：古国名，在今山东莒县，公元前431年被楚国消灭。〔8〕笃：厚。祜：福。〔9〕厥：指示代词，同"其"。〔10〕衡行：即"横行"。〔11〕今：如果，假如。

【译文】齐宣王问："与邻国结交有什么方法吗？"

孟子回答说："有。只有仁人才能以大国帮助小国，因此商汤帮助葛伯，周文王帮助昆夷；只有智者才能以小国的身份侍奉大国，因此周太王侍奉獯鬻，句践侍奉吴王夫差。以大国身份帮助小国的，是乐于听从天命的人；以小国身份侍奉大国的，是敬畏天命的人。乐于听从天命的人能安定天下，敬畏天命的人能安定自己的国家。《诗经》说：'敬畏上天的威灵，于是保有这个国家。'"

齐宣王说："讲得太好了！不过，我有个小毛病，就是逞强好勇。"

（孟子）回答说："那就请大王不要好小勇。有人按剑瞪眼，说：'他哪敢抵挡我！'这是匹夫之勇，只能对付一个人罢了。大王请把这样的勇扩大！《诗经》说：'文王勃然发怒，于是整顿军队，以阻挡侵犯莒国的敌军，以增厚周国的威福，以报答天下的期望。'这是周文王的勇。周文王发怒便使天下百姓都得到安定。《尚书》说：'上天降生万民，为他们设君主，立师长，要他们协助上天来宠爱四方百姓。所以，有罪者和无罪者，都由我来负责考察，普天之下，谁敢超越上天的意志？'所以，只要有一人在天下横行霸道，周武王便以此为耻。这就是武王的勇。周武王也是一怒而使天下百姓得到安定。如果大王也能做到一怒便使天下百姓得到安定，那么，老百姓就会唯恐大王不好勇了。"

【解读】孟子在本章阐发了两个方面的问题：一是如何处理好大国与小国之间的关系，二是何谓真正的勇，即大勇与小勇的区别。

大国与小国之间的和平相处，关乎黎民苍生安危，关乎家国社稷安危，统治者应高度重视和正确处理国家之间的关系，正所谓"外交无小事"。孟子认为国家有大小之分，国家之间的交往之道要讲究"仁"与"智"。大国面对小国要胸怀仁厚，有仁义之心，用仁德威服天下，修仁德以怀远人。小国应对大国要运用智慧，如句践事吴等，卑辞厚礼以求和，敬畏天命保其国。朱熹亦曰："天者，理而已矣。大之字小，小之事大，皆理之当然也。自然合理，故曰乐天，不敢违理，故曰畏天。包含遍覆，无不周遍，保天下之气象也。制节谨度，不敢纵逸，保一国之规模也。"

（朱熹《四书章句集注》）孟子心中对勇是持肯定态度的，但提倡要有大勇，即仁者之勇；反对小勇，即匹夫之勇。"小勇者，血气之怒也。大勇者，理义之怒也。血气之怒不可有，理义之怒不可无。知此，则可以见性情之正，而识天理人欲之分矣。"（朱熹《四书章句集注》）任气使强，即使如"力拔山兮气盖世"的项羽叱咤疆场，也是匹夫之勇。真正的勇应为仁者之勇、能安天下之勇，如文王、武王"一怒而安天下之民"。这种能护佑万民、安定苍生之勇，是充满仁义的勇，是孟子所赞赏的，百姓所期盼的。

2.4

　　齐宣王见孟子于雪宫[1]。王曰："贤者亦有此乐乎？"

　　孟子对曰："有。人不得，则非[2]其上矣。不得而非其上者，非也；为民上而不与民同乐者，亦非也。乐民之乐者，民亦乐其乐；忧民之忧者，民亦忧其忧。乐以天下，忧以天下，然而不王者，未之有也。

　　"昔者齐景公问于晏子曰：'吾欲观于转附、朝儛[3]，遵[4]海而南，放于琅邪。吾何修而可以比于先王观也？'

　　"晏子对曰：'善哉问也！天子适诸侯曰巡狩，巡狩者，巡所守也；诸侯朝于天子曰述职，述职者，述所职也。无非事者。春省耕而补不足，秋省敛而助不给。夏谚曰："吾王不游，吾何以休？吾王不豫[5]，吾何以助？一游一豫，为诸侯度。"今也不然：师行而粮食，饥者弗食，劳者弗息。睊睊胥谗[6]，民乃作慝[7]。方命[8]

虐民，饮食若流。流连荒亡，为诸侯忧。从流下而忘反谓之流，从流上而忘反谓之连，从兽无厌谓之荒，乐酒无厌谓之亡。先王无流连之乐，荒亡之行。惟君所行也。'

"景公说，大戒[9]于国，出舍于郊。于是始兴发补不足。召大师[10]曰：'为我作君臣相说之乐！'盖《徵招》《角招》是也。其诗曰：'畜君[11]何尤？'畜君者，好君也。"

The king Xuan of Qi had an interview with Mencius in the Snow palace, and said to him, "Do men of talents and worth likewise find pleasure in these things?"

Mencius replied, "They do; and if people generally are not able to enjoy themselves, they condemn their superiors. For them, when they cannot enjoy themselves, to condemn their superiors is wrong, but when the superiors of the people do not make enjoyment a thing common to the people and themselves, they also do wrong. When a ruler rejoices in the joy of his people, they also rejoice in his joy; when he grieves at the sorrow of his people, they also grieve at his sorrow. A sympathy of joy will pervade the kingdom; a sympathy of sorrow will do the same: —in such a state of things, it cannot be but that the ruler attain to the royal dignity.

Formerly, the duke Jing of Qi asked the minister Yan, saying, 'I wish to pay a visit of inspection to Zhuanfu, and Chaowu, and then to bend my course southward along the shore, till I come to Langya. What shall I do that my tour may be fit to be compared with the visits of inspection made by the ancient sovereigns?'

The minister Yan replied, 'An excellent inquiry! When the Son of Heaven visited the princes, it was called a tour of inspection, that is, be surveyed the states under their care. When the princes attended at the court of the Son of Heaven, it was called a report of office, that is, they reported their administration of their offices. Thus, neither of the proceedings was without a purpose. And moreover, in the spring they examined the ploughing, and supplied any deficiency of seed; in the autumn they examined the reaping, and supplied any deficiency of yield. There is the saying of the Xia dynasty, — If our king do not take his ramble, what will become of our happiness? If our king do not make his excursion, what will become of our help? That ramble, and that excursion, were a pattern to the princes. Now, the state of things is different. — A host marches in attendance on the ruler, and stores of provisions are consumed. The hungry are deprived of their food, and there is no rest for those who are called to toil. Maledictions are uttered by one to another with eyes askance, and the people proceed to the commission of wickedness. Thus the royal ordinances are violated, and the people are oppressed, and the supplies of food and drink flow away like water. The rulers yield themselves to the current, or they urge their way against it; they are wild; they are utterly lost: —these things proceed to the grief of the inferior princes. Descending along with the current, and forgetting to return, is what I call yielding to it. Pressing up against it, and forgetting to return, is what I call urging their way against it. Pursuing the chase without satiety is what I call being wild. Delighting in wine without satiety is what I call being lost. The ancient sovereigns had no pleasures to which they gave themselves as on the flowing stream; no doings which might be so characterized as wild and lost. It is for you, my prince, to pursue your course.'

The duke Ching was pleased. He issued a proclamation throughout his state, and went out and occupied a shed in the borders. From that time he began to open his granaries to supply the wants of the people, and calling the Grand music-master, he said to him, 'Make for me music to suit a prince and his minister pleased with each other.' And it was then that the *Zhishao* and *Jueshao* were made, in the words to which it was said, 'Is it a fault to restrain one's prince?' He who restrains his prince loves his prince."

【注释】［1］雪宫：齐国离宫，在今山东淄博东北。［2］非：非议，埋怨。［3］转附、朝儛(wǔ)：均为山名。[4]遵：沿着。[5]豫：专指君王出巡。［6］睊(juàn)睊：侧目相视。胥：皆，相互。谗：毁谤，说坏话。［7］慝(tè)：恶。[8]方命：逆王之命。方，逆。[9]戒：告命。［10］大师：即太师，古代的乐官。［11］畜(chù)君：朱熹《四书章句集注》解："言晏子能畜止其君之欲，宜为君之所尤，然其心则何过哉？"

【译文】齐宣王在雪宫接见孟子。宣王说："贤人也有在华丽的宫殿里居住游玩的快乐吗？"

孟子回答说："有。人们要是得不到这种快乐，就会埋怨他们的国君。得不到这种快乐就埋怨国君，是不对的；可是作为百姓的君主却不能与民同乐，也是不对的。国君如果以百姓的快乐为快乐，百姓也会以国君的快乐为快乐；国君如果以百姓的忧愁为忧愁，百姓也会以国君的忧愁为忧愁。以天下人的快乐为快乐，以天下人的忧愁为忧愁，这样还不能称王统一天下的，是从来没有的事。

"从前，齐景公问晏子说：'我想到转附、朝儛两座山去游玩，然后沿着海岸向南行，一直到琅邪。我该怎样做才能够和古代圣贤君王的巡游相比呢？'

"晏子回答说：'这个问题问得好呀！天子到诸侯国去叫作巡狩，巡狩就是巡视诸侯所守疆土；诸侯去朝见天子叫述职，述职就是报告在他职责内的工作。没有无事而空

樂以天下憂以天下

然而不王者未之有

也　語出孟子梁惠王下己亥秋仲亭書

录《孟子》句　张仲亭 书

行的。春天里巡视耕种情况，对粮食不够吃的给予补助；秋天里巡视收获情况，对歉收的给予补助。夏朝的谚语说："我王不出来游历，我怎么能得到休息？我王不出来巡视，我怎么能得到赏赐？一游一巡，足以作为诸侯的法度。"现在可不是这样了，国君一出游就兴师动众，索取粮食。饥饿的人得不到粮食补助，劳苦的人得不到休息。大家侧目而视，相互毁谤，并开始为非作歹。这种出游违背天意，虐待百姓，大吃大喝如同流水一样浪费。真是流连荒亡，连诸侯们都为此而忧虑。（什么叫流连荒亡呢？）从上游向下游游玩，乐而忘返叫作流；从下游向上游游玩，乐而忘返叫作连；打猎不知节制叫作荒；嗜酒不加节制叫作亡。古代圣贤君王既无流连的享乐，也无荒亡的行为。至于大王您的行为，只有您自己选择了。'

"齐景公（听了晏子的话）非常高兴，先大张旗鼓地向全国发布告命，然后驻扎在

郊外，打开仓库赈济贫困的百姓。又召集乐
官说：'请为我创作一些君臣同乐的乐曲！'
因此就有了《徵招》《角招》。其中的歌词说：
'畜君有什么不对呢？'畜君，就是爱戴国
君的意思。"

【解读】湖南岳阳楼有一副名联："四面湖山
归眼底，万家忧乐到心头。"或言执政者居
庙堂之高，要多关注苍生疾苦，万家忧乐。
这副对联与范仲淹的名句"先天下之忧而忧，
后天下之乐而乐"有异曲同工之妙，所蕴含
的思想与情怀大概皆出自孟子在本章中表达
的观点"乐以天下，忧以天下"。孟子在这
里倡导的还是与民同乐、与民同忧的"仁政"
理念，他通过与齐宣王的雪宫之游，来劝诫
其不应沉溺于物欲享乐之中，应"乐民之
乐""忧民之忧"。然后以齐景公与晏子的
对话为例，进一步论证了其中的道理。朱熹
曰："人君能与民同乐，则人皆有此乐。不然，

齐宣王见孟子于雪宫　杨晓刚　绘

则下之不得此乐者，必有非其君上之心。明人君当与民同乐，不可使人有不得者，非但当与贤者共之而已也。"（朱熹《四书章句集注》）这也鲜明地体现了孟子的民本思想。

如果当政者只是享受一己的欢乐，一味地声色犬马，且不懂得节制，人民就会不满他们的国君，国家将衰亡。历史上这些反面的事例不胜枚举，如商纣王、秦二世、隋炀帝等无不如此流连荒亡，奢靡无度。如何杜绝这样的现象发生呢？孟子主张"畜君"，就是让国君受到一定的限制和约束，正如朱熹所言："臣能畜止其君之欲，乃是爱其君者也。"（朱熹《四书章句集注》）

2.5

齐宣王问曰："人皆谓我毁明堂[1]。毁诸？已乎？"

孟子对曰："夫明堂者，王者之堂也。王欲行王政，则勿毁之矣。"

王曰："王政可得闻与？"

对曰："昔者文王之治岐也，耕者九一[2]，仕者世禄，关市讥[3]而不征，泽梁[4]无禁，罪人不孥[5]。老而无妻曰鳏。老而无夫曰寡。老而无子曰独。幼而无父曰孤。此四者，天下之穷民而无告者。文王发政施仁，必先斯四者。《诗》云：'哿矣富人，哀此茕独[6]。'"

王曰："善哉言乎！"

曰："王如善之，则何为不行？"

王曰："寡人有疾，寡人好货。"

对曰："昔者公刘好货。《诗》云：'乃积乃仓，乃裹糇粮[7]，于橐于囊[8]。思戢[9]用光。弓矢斯张，干戈戚扬，爰方启行[10]。'

故居者有积仓，行者有裹粮也，然后可以爱
方启行。王如好货，与百姓同之，于王何有？"

王曰："寡人有疾，寡人好色。"

对曰："昔者大王好色，爱厥[11]妃。《诗》
云：'古公亶甫，来朝走马，率西水浒[12]，
至于岐下。爱及姜女，聿来胥宇[13]。'当是
时也，内无怨女，外无旷夫[14]。王如好色，
与百姓同之，于王何有？"

The king Xuan of Qi said, "People all tell me
to pull down and remove the Hall of Distinction.
Shall I pull it down, or stop the movement for that
object?"

Mencius replied, "The Hall of Distinction is a
Hall appropriate to the sovereigns. If Your Majesty
wishes to practise the true royal government, then
do not pull it down."

The king said, "May I hear from you what the
true royal government is?"

"Formerly," was the reply, "king Wen's government of Qi was as follows: —The husbandmen cultivated for the government one- ninth of the land; the descendants of officers were salaried; at the passes and in the markets, strangers were inspected, but goods were not taxed: there were no prohibitions respecting the ponds and weirs; the wives and children of criminals were not involved in their guilt. There were the old and wifeless, or widowers; the old and husbandless, or widows; the old and childless, or solitaries; the young and fatherless, or orphans: —these four classes are the most destitute of the people, and have none to whom they can tell their wants, and king Wen, in the institution of his government with its benevolent action, made them the first objects of his regard, as it is said in the *Book of Poetry*, 'The rich may get through life well; But alas! for the miserable and solitary!'"

The king said, "O excellent words!"

Mencius said, "Since Your Majesty deems them excellent, why do you not practise them?"

"I have an infirmity," said the king. "I am fond of wealth."

The reply was, "Formerly, Gong Liu was fond of wealth. It is said in the *Book of Poetry*, 'He reared his ricks, and filled his granaries, He tied up dried provisions and grain, In bottomless bags, and sacks, That he might gather his people together, and glorify his State. With bows and arrows all-displayed, With shields, and spears, and battle-axes, large and small, He commenced his march.' In this way those who remained in their old seat had their ricks and granaries, and those who marched had their bags of provisions. It was not till after this that he thought he could begin his march. If Your Majesty loves wealth, give the people power to gratify the same feeling, and what difficulty will there be in your attaining the royal sway?"

The king said, "I have an infirmity; I am fond of beauty."

The reply was, "Formerly, king Tai was fond of beauty, and loved his wife. It is said in the *Book of Poetry*, '*Gugong Danfu*, Came in the morning, galloping his horse, By the banks of the western waters, As far as the foot of Qi hill, Along with the lady of Jiang; They came and together chose the site for their settlement.' At that time, in the seclusion of the house, there were no dissatisfied women, and abroad, there were no unmarried men. If Your Majesty loves beauty, let the people be able to gratify the same feeling, and what difficulty will there be in your attaining the royal sway?"

【注释】［1］明堂：天子接见诸侯、处理政务的场所。此处指泰山明堂。［2］耕者九一：指井田制。将农田分成井字，每井九百亩，周围八家各一百亩，属私田，中间一百亩属公田，由八家共同耕种，收成充为公粮，因此称作九一税制。〔3〕讥：稽查，盘问。〔4〕泽梁：在流水中用来拦水捕鱼的装置。〔5〕不孥（nú）：不连累妻子儿女。孥：原指妻子儿女，名词活用作动词。〔6〕哿（gě）矣富人，哀此茕独：引自《诗经·小雅·正月》。哿：欢乐。茕：无依无靠。〔7〕糇（hóu）粮：外出之人随身携带的吃食，干粮。〔8〕于橐（tuó）于囊：橐和囊是两种盛东西的器物，囊大橐小。〔9〕戢（jí）：同"辑"，安辑，和睦。〔10〕爰：于是，就。启行：动身启程。〔11〕厥（jué）：代词，他的，那个。〔12〕率：沿着。浒：水边。〔13〕聿：语首词，无义。胥：动词，省视，视察。〔14〕旷夫：无妻男子。

【译文】齐宣王问（孟子）说："别人都劝谏我拆毁明堂，我是把它拆掉呢，还是保留下来呢？"

孟子回答说："明堂是王者施行王政的殿堂。大王若想施行王政，那么还是不要拆毁它。"

齐宣王说："关于王政，能说给我听听吗？"

（孟子）回答说："从前周文王治理岐山时，对农民实行九一税制，做官的人世代承袭俸禄，在关卡和市场方面只稽查而不征税，任何人到湖泊捕鱼都不被禁止，对于犯罪的人的处罚不牵连妻子儿女。年老无妻叫鳏，年老无夫叫寡，年老无儿女叫独，幼年无父母叫孤。这四种人是天下贫困潦倒孤独无依的人，文王施行仁政，一定最先考虑到这四种人。《诗经》说：'欢乐的富人都生活得很好，可怜那些孤独穷苦无依无靠的人。'"

齐宣王说："说得对呀！"

（孟子）说："大王如果认为说得对，为什么不那么做呢？"

齐宣王说："我有个缺点，我贪好财物。"

　　（孟子）说："从前公刘也爱好钱财，《诗经》说：'粮食积满仓，裹好干粮，装满袋囊，和谐一致奔向好时光。箭上弦，弓开张，盾戈斧钺都带上，起身前行向远方。'所以，留在家里的人有积累的余粮，外出的人有足够的干粮，这才可以动身出发。大王若贪好财物，能和百姓同享，这对于施行王政，有什么困难呢？"

　　齐宣王说："我还有个缺点，我贪恋女色。"

　　（孟子）回答说："从前周太王也爱好女色，非常爱他的妃子。《诗经》说：'周太王古公亶甫，骑着快马，沿着西边河岸，到达岐山下面，带着妻子姜氏女，察看地形，修建屋宇。'当时家中没有嫁不出去的哀怨女，外面也没有娶不到妻子的单身汉。大王如果爱好女色，应该想到百姓也爱好女色，这对于施行王政有什么困难呢？"

【解读】本章孟子利用齐宣王要不要拆毁明堂之问，来劝诫宣王"欲行王政，则勿毁之矣"。孟子的"王政"以周文王为例，就是要求执政者要有仁爱之心，能够推己及人，体恤黎民百姓之苦，照顾老弱病残等社会弱势群体。

　　齐宣王对孟子的"仁政"大加称赞，但他提出了两个纠结的问题：寡人好货与好色。在那个寡廉鲜耻、天下动荡的战国时代，这样的行为在天下大行其道。然而孟子顺势开导齐宣王，借助公刘和古公亶甫的历史事例，宣讲自己的主张，认为"好货""好色"皆是人之常情，为人之正常需求。但公刘和古公亶甫能够将心比心，用自己的所好之心体恤百姓之所好，己所欲，施于人，"与百姓同之"，这就体现出"好货""好色"与施行王政并不冲突。当然孟子的意思并不是"好货""好色"都可以满足，他其实坚持的是儒家的道义，希望统治者去施行仁政。

2.6

孟子谓齐宣王曰："王之臣有托其妻子于其友，而之楚游者。比其反也[1]，则[2]冻馁其妻子，则如之何？"

王曰："弃之。"

曰："士师不能治士，则如之何？"

王曰："已[3]之。"

曰："四境之内不治，则如之何？"

王顾左右而言他。

Mencius said to the king Xuan of Qi, "Suppose that one of Your Majesty's ministers were to entrust his wife and children to the care of his friend, while he himself went into Chu to travel, and that, on his return, he should find that the friend had let his wife and children suffer from cold and hunger; —how ought he to deal with him?"

The king said, "He should cast him off."

Mencius proceeded, "Suppose that the chief criminal judge could not regulate the officers under him, how would you deal with him?"

The king said, "Dismiss him."

Mencius again said, "If within the four borders of your kingdom there is not good government, what is to be done?"

The king looked to the right and left, and spoke of other matters.

【注释】[1]比(bǐ): 及, 至, 等到。反: 同"返"。[2]则: 表结果, 结果是。[3]已: 止, 指罢免。

【译文】孟子对齐宣王说: "若大王的臣子中有一个将妻子儿女托寄给他的朋友照看, 而他到楚国游历。等到他返回来后, 结果发现妻子儿女挨饿受冻, 这样, 该如何办?"

齐宣王说: "抛弃他。"

(孟子)说: "如果司法官不能管理好

他的属下，那该如何办？"

齐宣王说："撤他的职。"

（孟子又）说："如果一个国家治理得不安定，那又该如何办？"

齐宣王环顾左右，把话题扯开了。

【解读】本章孟子运用归谬和类比的论证方式，由浅入深，从臣子不能照顾好友人妻子的小事，到"士师不能治士"，再到王的"四境之内不治"，用这一相通的逻辑来教化齐宣王，体现了孟子鲜明的思辨个性。朱熹曰："孟子将问此而先设上二事以发之，及此而王不能答也。其惮于自责，耻于下问如此，不足与有为可知矣。"（朱熹《四书章句集注》）孟子用这种归谬的论证方式，引导齐宣王一步步进入自己的理论包围圈，从而让他明白施行"仁政"的重要意义。最精彩的是末尾的一句"王顾左右而言他"，逼得齐宣王无言以对，体现了孟子说理论辩的高超技巧。

2.7

孟子见齐宣王曰："所谓故国^[1]者，非谓有乔木之谓也，有世臣^[2]之谓也。王无亲臣矣，昔者所进^[3]，今日不知其亡^[4]也。"

王曰："吾何以识其不才而舍之？"

曰："国君进贤，如不得已，将使卑逾尊，疏逾戚^[5]，可不慎与？左右皆曰贤，未可也；诸大夫皆曰贤，未可也；国人皆曰贤，然后察之，见贤焉，然后用之。左右皆曰不可，勿听；诸大夫皆曰不可，勿听；国人皆曰不可，然后察之，见不可焉，然后去之。左右皆曰可杀，勿听；诸大夫皆曰可杀，勿听；国人皆曰可杀，然后察之，见可杀焉，然后杀之。故曰，国人杀之也。如此，然后可以为民父母。"

Mencius, having an interview with the king Xuan of Qi, said to him, "When men speak of 'an ancient kingdom', it is not meant thereby that it has lofty trees in it, but that it has ministers sprung from families which have been noted in it for generations. Your Majesty has no intimate ministers even. Those whom you advanced yesterday are gone today, and you do not know it."

The king said, "How shall I know that they have not ability, and so avoid employing them at all?"

The reply was, "The ruler of a State advances to office men of talents and virtue only as a matter of necessity. Since he will thereby cause the low to overstep the honourable, and distant to overstep his near relatives, ought he to do so but with caution? When all those about you say, 'This is a man of talents and worth,' you may not therefore believe it. When your great officers all say, 'This is a man of talents and virtue,' neither may you for that believe it. When all the people say, 'This is a man of talents and virtue,' then examine into the case, and when you find that the man is such, employ him. When all those about you say, 'This man won't do,' don't listen to them. When all your great officers say, 'This man won't do,' don't listen to them. When the people all say, 'This man won't do,' then examine into the case, and when you find that the man won't do, send him away. When all those about you say, 'This man deserves death,' don't listen to them. When all your great officers say, 'This man deserves death,' don't listen to them. When the people all say, 'This man deserves death,' then inquire into the case, and when you see that the man deserves death, put him to death. In accordance with this we have the saying, 'The people killed him.' You must act in this way in order to be the parent of the people."

【注释】［1］故国：指历史悠久的国家。［2］世臣：世代建立功勋的大臣。［3］进：进用。［4］亡：去位，去职。［5］疏：疏远。戚：

亲近，亲密。

【译文】孟子谒见齐宣王，说："我们所说的历史悠久的国家，并不是说国家有高大的树木，而是说有世代建立功勋的大臣。可大王您现在没有可以亲信的臣子了，过去任用的人，现在也不知为什么离去了。"

齐宣王说："我怎样才能辨识出那些没有真正才能的人而舍弃他们呢？"

（孟子）说："国君选拔贤能，若在不得已的情况下，会把地位卑贱的人提拔到地位高的人之上，把关系疏远的人提拔到关系亲近的人之上，能不谨慎吗？左右侍从都说某人好，不能轻易相信；众大夫都说某人好，也不能轻易相信；全国的人都说某人好，然后再考察他，发现他真的是贤才，再任用他。左右侍从都说某人不好，不要听信；众大夫都说某人不好，也不要轻易听信；全国的人都说某人不好，然后去考察他，发现他真的不好，再罢免他。左右侍从都说某人该杀，不可听信；众大夫都说某人该杀，不可听信；全国的人都说某人该杀，然后去考察他，发现他真的该杀，再杀掉他。因此说，是国民杀的他。只有这样，才可以做百姓的父母官。"

【解读】古语云："千金易得，一将难求。"极言人才的重要性。怎样识别选拔人才呢？本章孟子就阐发了这一问题。

孟子对人才极为重视，尤其是治国理政的济世之才，孟子强调的是选贤任能。所以他曾说一个历史久远的国家最重要的是要有世勋之臣，即能为国家建立功勋、与国家休戚与共的臣子。那么如何甄别贤明之士并选拔出来呢？在孟子看来，人才的任用"如不得已，将使卑逾尊，疏逾戚"，同时还应注意，兼听则明，偏信则暗的问题，无论是选贤，还是罢免不称职者，抑或惩办罪臣，都要广泛听取广大民众的评判。朱熹曰："故必自察之，而亲见其贤否之实，然后从而用舍之；则于贤者知之深，任之重，而不才者不得以幸进矣。所谓进贤如不得已者如此。"（朱熹《四书章句集注》）从朱熹的评述可以看出孟子选拔人才的原则：一个人是否贤能，是否进用，不能偏听偏信近臣和士大夫等少数人的意见，要广泛倾听社会各方面的意见，还要居上位者亲自去考察，确认其贤能与否。这就是尊重民意。当今现实社会，在选拔任用干部的工作中，孟子所主张的考察方法，至今仍然具有重要借鉴意义和实践价值。

2.8

齐宣王问曰："汤放桀，武王伐纣，有诸？"

孟子对曰："于传[1] 有之。"

曰："臣弑[2] 其君可乎？"

曰："贼仁者谓之贼，贼义者谓之残，残贼之人谓之一夫[3]。闻诛一夫纣矣，未闻弑君也。"

The king Xuan of Qi asked, saying, "Was it so, that Tang banished Jie, and that king Wu smote Zhou?"

Mencius replied, "It is so in the records."

The king said, "May a minister then put his sovereign to death?"

Mencius said, "He who outrages the benevolence proper to his nature, is called a robber; he who outrages righteousness, is called a ruffian. The robber and ruffian we call a mere fellow. I have heard of the cutting off of the fellow Zhou, but I have not heard of the putting a sovereign to death, in his case."

【注释】［1］传：书传，书籍。［2］弑：特指居下位者杀在上位者。［3］一夫：匹夫，独夫。

【译文】齐宣王问孟子说："商汤流放夏桀，武王讨伐纣王，有这回事吗？"

孟子答道："书传中有这种记载。"

（齐宣王）问："臣子杀掉君主，可以吗？"

（孟子）说："伤害仁德的人叫作贼，伤害正义的人叫作残，残和贼之类的人被称作独夫。听说过诛杀了独夫纣，没有听说过这是弑君。"

【解读】孟子本章中讨论了取得政权的合法性问题。儒家历来重视名分，君权的取得亦当合乎名分，否则就属于乱臣贼子的违礼行为。

儒家历来讲究"君权天授"，帝王是天子，代表上天来管理天下，帝王如果干得不好，会受到上天的惩罚谴责。所以关于"汤放桀，武王伐纣"是否合理合法的问题，孟子与齐宣王在认识上产生了分歧。虽然夏桀与商纣王残暴无道，在齐宣王看来，他们的身份乃是天子，商汤和周武王是犯上作乱，是"臣弑其君"，那么政权的获取就是非法的。孟子在这一点上的认识更为进步，朱熹评价说："害仁者，凶暴淫虐，灭绝天理，故谓之贼。害义者，颠倒错乱，伤败彝伦，故谓之残。一夫，言众叛亲离，不复以为君也。""盖四海归之，则为天子；天下叛之，则为独夫。所以深警齐王，垂戒后世也。"（朱熹《四书章句集注》）孟子认为，不仁者、害义者，即便贵为天子，若不能尽为君之责，残仁害义，是为独夫民贼，是可以诛杀的。孟子明确肯定了推翻暴君的合理合法性，这种思想具有巨大的历史进步意义。

2.9

　　孟子见齐宣王曰："为巨室，则必使工师求大木。工师得大木，则王喜，以为能胜其任也。匠人斫[1]而小之，则王怒，以为不胜其任矣。夫人幼而学之，壮而欲行之。王曰'姑舍女所学而从我'，则何如？今有璞玉于此，虽万镒[2]，必使玉人雕琢之。至于治国家，则曰'姑舍女所学而从我'，则何以异于教玉人雕琢玉哉？"

Mencius, having an interview with the king Xuan of Qi, said to him, "If you are going to build a large mansion, you will surely cause the Master of the workmen to look out for large trees, and when he has found such large trees, you will be glad, thinking that they will answer for the intended object. Should the workmen hew them so as to make them too small, then Your Majesty will be angry, thinking that they will not answer for the purpose. Now, a man spends his youth in learning the principles of right government, and, being grown up to vigour, he wishes to put them in practice; if Your Majesty says to him, 'For the present put aside what you have learned, and follow me,' what shall we say? Here now you have a gem unwrought, in the stone. Although it may be worth 240,000 taels, you will surely employ a lapidary to cut and polish it. But when you come to the government of the State, then you say, 'For the present put aside what you have learned, and follow me.' How is it that you herein act so differently from your conduct in calling in the lapidary to cut the gem?"

【注释】［1］斫（zhuó）：砍，削。［2］镒（yì）：古代重量单位，二十两（一说二十四两）为一镒。

【译文】孟子拜见齐宣王说："建造大宫室，就一定要叫工师去寻找大木料。工师找到了大木料，大王就高兴，认为他可以胜任其职。木匠砍削木料，把木料砍小了，大王就会发怒，认为木匠不能胜任其职。有人从小就学习，长大后想实践其所学本领。大王却说'暂且放弃你所学的，听从我的'，这会怎么样？设想现在有块璞玉在这里，即使价值万金，也一定会叫制玉人来雕琢加工。至于治理国家，却说'暂且放弃你所学的，听从我的'，那么，这和您要玉匠按您的办法去雕琢玉石有什么不同呢？"

【解读】本章中齐宣王与孟子讨论了用权力治国还是用专业治国的问题。孟子用建造大的宫殿，一定请专业大师来设计和寻找建造宫殿的大木来做类比，又用玉匠雕琢价值万镒的璞玉进一步作类比阐发齐宣王不能真正地尊重人才，用其所长，只是要求人才"姑舍女所学而从我", 以致外行领导内行、专长服从权力, 造成资源浪费、人才废弛的结果。孟子的意思是国家需要的不是顺从国君意愿的宠臣, 而是治国安邦的栋梁之臣、专业之臣。治理国家要任用贤才并尊重他们的技能, 而不能运用国君的强权让所有人听从自己, 屈从于权力。北宋范祖禹说: "古之贤者, 常患人君不能行其所学; 而世之庸君, 亦常患贤者不能从其所好。是以君臣相遇, 自古以为难。孔孟终身而不遇, 盖以此耳。"(朱熹《四书章句集注》)范氏就深深忧虑国君不能充分认清并发挥人才的优长, 而那些庸君更是要求贤能之人顺其所愿, 投其所好, 因此那种"君使臣以礼, 臣事君以忠"的君臣相谐、齐心共治的美好君臣关系, 更是可遇不可求。

2.10

　　齐人伐燕，胜之。宣王问曰："或谓寡人勿取，或谓寡人取之。以万乘之国伐万乘之国，五旬而举之，人力不至于此。不取，必有天殃。取之，何如？"

　　孟子对曰："取之而燕民悦，则取之。古之人有行之者，武王是也。取之而燕民不悦，则勿取。古之人有行之者，文王是也。以万乘之国伐万乘之国，箪食[1]壶浆以迎王师。岂有他哉？避水火也。如水益深，如火益热，亦运[2]而已矣。"

The people of Qi attacked Yan, and conquered it. The king Xuan asked, saying, "Some tell me not to take possession of it for myself, and some tell me to take possession of it. For a kingdom of ten thousand chariots, attacking another of ten thousand chariots, to complete the conquest of it in fifty days, is an achievement beyond mere human strength. If I do not take possession of it, calamities from Heaven will surely come upon me. What do you say to my taking possession of it?"

Mencius replied, "If the people of Yan will be pleased with your taking possession of it, then do so. Among the ancients there was one who acted on this principle, namely king Wu. If the people of Yan will not be pleased with your taking possession of it, then do not do so. Among the ancients there was one who acted on this principle, namely king Wen. When, with all the strength of your country of ten thousand chariots, you attacked another country of ten thousand chariots, and the people brought baskets of rice and vessels of congee, to meet Your Majesty's host, was there any other reason for this but that they hoped to escape out of fire and water? If you make the water more deep and the fire more fierce, they will in like manner make another revolution."

【注释】［1］箪：盛饭的竹筐。食：饭。［2］
运：改变，转变。

【译文】齐国人讨伐燕国，齐国取得胜利。齐
宣王问（孟子）说："有人劝我不要占领燕国，
有人又劝我占领它。用一个拥有万辆兵车的
大国去讨伐一个同样拥有万辆兵车的大国，
五十天就攻打成功了，凭借人力是达不到这
个地步的。若不占领它，必定会遇到天灾。
占领它，会怎么样啊？"

孟子回答说："占领它而使燕国的子民
感到高兴，那么就占领它。古代有这样做的人，
周武王便是。占领它而使燕国的子民不高兴，
那么就不要占领它。古代有这样做的人，周
文王便是。凭一个拥有万辆兵车的齐国去讨
伐同样拥有万辆兵车的燕国，燕国的百姓如
果能用篮子装着干粮，用壶盛着汤汁来欢迎
大王您的军队，难道还有其他原因吗？是想
逃离那种水深火热的日子罢了。如果他们的

生活像水一样更深，像火一样更热，那他们也会转过头来去寻求别的出路了。"

【解读】齐人伐燕之事发生于公元前 314 年，燕王哙效仿尧舜，以禅让的形式将国君之位让于相国子之。国人不服，燕国政局陷入混乱中。齐宣王趁机出兵攻打燕国，结果燕国"士卒不战，城门不闭"，齐军五旬而取燕国。齐宣王有意说这是天意，违背天意将遭受上天惩罚，实为窃取燕国找寻借口。其实齐宣王未真知天意，是以其私欲为天意。

孟子不反对武力征伐，他认为征伐只要顺应民心，合乎民意，那么民心则大悦，民心喜悦则天意得，天意得就可以占领别人的国家。孟子对天意的理解，有着清晰的认识：谁能够解民于倒悬，救民于水火，谁就能获取百姓的支持，燕国百姓的悦与不悦，是决定天意的基础。所以孟子认为民心就是天意，能不能得到燕国之地，取决于燕国民心。

2.11

齐人伐燕，取之。诸侯将谋救燕。宣王曰：
"诸侯多谋伐寡人者，何以待之？"

孟子对曰："臣闻七十里为政于天下者，
汤是也。未闻以千里畏人者也。《书》曰：'汤
一征，自葛始。'天下信之。'东面而征，西
夷怨；南面而征，北狄怨。曰，奚为后我？'
民望之，若大旱之望云霓也。归市者[1] 不止，
耕者不变。诛其君而吊[2] 其民，若时雨降，
民大悦。《书》曰：'徯我后[3]，后来其苏[4]。'
今燕虐其民，王往而征之。民以为将拯己于水
火之中也，箪食壶浆，以迎王师。若杀其父兄，
系累[5] 其子弟，毁其宗庙，迁其重器，如之
何其可也？天下固畏齐之强也。今又倍地而不
行仁政，是动天下之兵也。王速出令，反其旄
倪[6]，止其重器，谋于燕众，置君而后去之，
则犹可及止也。"

The people of Qi, having smitten Yan, took possession of it, and upon this, the princes of the various States deliberated together, and resolved to deliver Yan from their power. The king Xuan said to Mencius, "The princes have formed many plans to attack me—how shall I prepare myself for them?"

Mencius replied, "I have heard of one who with seventy *li* exercised all the functions of government throughout the kingdom. That was Tang. I have never heard of a prince with a thousand *li* standing in fear of others. It is said in the *Book of History*, As soon as Tang began his work of executing justice, he commenced with Ge. The whole kingdom had confidence in him. When he pursued his work in the east, the rude tribes on the west murmured. So did those on the north, when he was engaged in the south. Their cry was 'Why does he put us last?' Thus, the people looked to him, as we look in a time of great drought to the clouds and rainbows. The frequenters of the markets stopped not. The husbandmen made no change in their operations. While he punished their rulers, he consoled the people. His progress was like the falling of opportune rain, and the people were delighted. It is said again in the *Book of History*, 'We have waited for our prince long; the prince's coming will be our reviving!' "Now the ruler of Yan was tyrannizing over his people, and Your Majesty went and punished him. The people supposed that you were going to deliver them out of the water and the fire, and brought baskets of rice and vessels of congee, to meet Your Majesty's host. But you have slain their fathers and elder brothers, and put their sons and younger brothers in confinement. You have pulled down the ancestral temple of the State, and are removing to Qi its precious vessels. How can such a course be deemed proper? The rest of the kingdom is indeed jealously afraid of the strength of Qi; and now, when with a doubled territory you do not put in practice a benevolent government — it is this which sets the arms of the kingdom in in motion. If Your Majesty will make haste to issue an ordinance, restoring your captives, old and young, stopping the removal of the precious vessels, and saying that, after consulting with the people of Yen, you will appoint them a ruler, and withdraw from the country — in this way you may still be able to stop the threatened attack."

【注释】[1] 归市者：指做生意的人。[2] 吊：安抚，慰问。[3] 徯（xī）：等待。后：王，君主。[4] 后来其苏：君王来了，我们就会复苏、复活。[5] 系累：束缚，捆绑。[6] 旄（mào）倪：旄，通"耄"，八九十岁的人叫耄，指老年人。倪：指小孩子。

【译文】齐人攻打燕国，占领了它。一些诸侯

国就谋划着救助燕国。齐宣王说："许多诸
侯谋划着来攻打我，这该怎么对付他们？"

　　孟子回答说："我听说过凭借着方圆
七十里的土地能统一天下的，那就是商汤。
没有听说过以方圆千里的大国却害怕别人的。
《尚书》说：'商汤初征，从葛国开始。'
天下人都相信他是为铲除暴政而来。'当他
向东方进攻时，西方各族的百姓就抱怨；当
他向南方进攻时，北方各族的百姓就抱怨，
都说，为什么把我们放到后面呢？'百姓都
盼望，就像大旱盼乌云和虹霓一样。做生意
的正常经营，种地的正常劳作。商汤只是杀
掉残暴的君主而抚恤百姓，就像及时雨从天
而降，百姓非常高兴。《尚书》说：'等待
我们的王，王来了我们就复活了。'现在燕
国的君主虐待百姓，大王您的军队去讨伐他。
燕国的百姓都认为您是要从水深火热中将他
们解救出来，便都用篮子盛着饭，用壶盛着
汤来欢迎您的军队。但您若杀死他们的父兄，拘囚他们的子弟，拆毁他们的宗庙，抢走他们的宝器，那怎么能行呢？天下诸侯本来就畏惧齐国的强盛。如今齐国的土地又扩张了一倍却不施行仁政，这必定会激起天下动兵。大王应该马上颁布政令，把燕国老年人和小孩放回，停止抢掠宝器，并和燕国民众商讨，帮助他们重立一位国君后撤回齐国军队。这样做，还来得及阻止各国动兵。"

【解读】上一章齐宣王询问孟子占领燕国的事宜，齐军攻占燕国以后，实力似乎更加强大，骤然之间成为东方国土面积最大的国家。齐国本来成就过王霸之业，此时齐宣王风头正盛，一时无人能出其右，天下平衡的态势被打破，这成了诸侯大国的忧患，小国的忧惧。由是各诸侯国打着挽救燕国的旗号，谋划着讨伐齐国。

齐宣王赶紧问计于孟子，寻求应对之策。孟子趁机继续说服齐宣王施行仁政。北宋范祖禹评述此事："孟子事齐梁之君，论道德则必称尧舜，论征伐则必称汤武。盖治民不法尧舜，则是为暴；行师不法汤武，则是为乱。岂可谓吾君不能，而舍所学以徇之哉？"（朱熹《四书章句集注》）范氏的观点与孟子高度一致，认为如不效法汤武征伐，则是为乱于天下，所以商汤能以区区方圆七十里之地统一天下，其征伐四方，天下之民皆翘首以盼，黎民百姓期待商汤的义军如久旱企望甘霖一样。

　　强大的齐国王师到达燕国之初，燕民也"箪食壶浆以迎王师"，最终因齐军贪婪残暴的不仁行为引动天下之兵将伐齐，何也？相似的情形在后世也再次上演，明末李自成率领义军挥师进京，京城之民也"箪食壶浆以迎王师"，可是由于李自成纵容手下将士抢掠百姓，贪于美色财货，军纪涣散，起义军失去民心，导致李自成狼狈退出京师，亡命天涯，命丧九宫山。齐宣王与李自成有着

惊人相似的一点，就是使占领地的人民陷于
更深的水深火热之中。征伐未能顺应民意，
施政不能得到民心，不得民心怎能得天下？

2.12

邹与鲁哄 [1]。穆公问曰："吾有司死者三十三人，而民莫之死 [2] 也。诛之，则不可胜诛；不诛，则疾 [3] 视其长上之死而不救，如之何则可也？"

孟子对曰："凶年饥岁，君之民老弱转 [4] 乎沟壑，壮者散而之四方者，几 [5] 千人矣；而君之仓廪实，府库充，有司莫以告，是上慢 [6] 而残下也。曾子曰：'戒之戒之！出乎尔者，反乎尔者也。'夫民今而后得反之也。君无尤 [7] 焉。君行仁政，斯民亲其上、死其长矣。"

There had been a brush between Zou and Lu, when the duke Mu asked Mencius, saying, "Of my officers there were killed thirty-three men, and none of the people would die in their defence. Though I sentenced them to death for their conduct, it is impossible to put such a multitude to death. If I do not put them to death, then there is the crime unpunished of their looking angrily on at the death of their officers, and not saving them. How is the exigency of the case to be met?"

Mencius replied, "In calamitous years and years of famine, the old and weak of your people, who have been found lying in the ditches and water channels, and the able-bodied who have been scattered about to the four quarters, have amounted to several thousands. All the while, your granaries, O prince, have been stored with grain, and your treasuries and arsenals have been full, and not one of your officers has told you of the distress. Thus negligent have the superiors in your State been, and cruel to their inferiors. The philosopher Zeng said, 'Beware, beware. What proceeds from you, will return to you again.' Now at length the people have paid back the conduct of their officers to them. Do not you, O prince, blame them. If you will put in practice a benevolent government, this people will love you and all above them, and will die for their officers."

【注释】［1］哄（hòng）：争斗，交战。［2］莫之死：意思是没有人为他们而死。［3］疾：憎恨。［4］转：辗转，指因饥饿辗转而死。［5］几：近。［6］慢：怠慢。［7］尤：动词，责备，归罪。

【译文】邹国与鲁国交战。邹穆公对（孟子）说："我的官吏死了三十三个，然而没有一个百姓愿为他们去牺牲。把他们杀掉，无法杀尽；不杀他们，又憎恨他们眼看着长官被杀却不解救，该怎么办才好呢？"

孟子说："灾荒年月时，您的百姓，年老体弱者因饥饿辗转而死在山野沟壑里，身强体壮者便逃散四方，应该有近千人吧；而您的粮仓里有充足的粮食，府库里有充足的财物，官吏们不把这情况向您禀告，这是上位者怠慢而残害百姓啊。曾子说：'小心啊，小心啊！你怎样对待别人，别人也会怎样对待你。'现在到了百姓反击他们的时候了。您不要归罪于百姓。君王您如果施行仁政，那么百姓就会亲近他们的长官，愿意为长官而死。"

【解读】孟子在很多场合进行辩论时，常常采用类比推理、巧用比喻、由远及近、循循善诱等方式进行说理和论辩。而这一次在与邹穆公的答问中，孟子一反往常，直截了当地回应邹穆公的尖锐问题。

本章中孟子通过邹鲁两国战争阐述了国家对百姓、官员对百姓的做法而产生的后果，问题的实质还是执政者能否施行仁政，百姓和官员与国家能否上下一心。在邹与鲁的交战中，百姓对官员在战场上的伤亡漠不关心，邹穆王非常恼火，想要惩罚百姓。孟子一针

见血地指出，灾荒之年，百姓饿毙或流离失
所时，官员们见死不救，冷漠面对民众水深
火热的处境，仁义何在？温情何在？北宋范
祖禹说："有仓廪府库，所以为民也。丰年
则敛之，凶年则散之，恤其饥寒，救其疾苦。
是以民亲爱其上，有危难则赴救之，如子弟
之卫父兄，手足之捍头目也。穆公不能反己，
犹欲归罪于民，岂不误哉？"（朱熹《四书
章句集注》）从范氏的言论可以看出，百姓
是一国之本，执政者要体恤百姓，尤其是饥
荒之年，为官以仁，施政以仁，情系民生疾苦，
那么百姓就能与君王社稷上下同心。

2.13

滕文公问曰："滕，小国也，间[1]于齐、楚。事齐乎？事楚乎？"

孟子对曰："是谋非吾所能及也。无已[2]，则有一焉：凿斯池[3]也，筑斯城也，与民守之，效[4]死而民弗去，则是可为也。"

The duke Wen of Teng asked Mencius, saying, "Teng is a small kingdom, and lies between Qi and Chu. Shall I serve Qi? Or shall I serve Chu?"

Mencius replied, "This plan which you propose is beyond me. If you will have me counsel you, there is one thing I can suggest. Dig deeper your moats; build higher your walls; guard them as well as your people. In case of attack, be prepared to die in your defence, and have the people so that they will not leave you; —this is a proper course."

【注释】［1］间（jiàn）：夹处。［2］无已：
不得已。［3］池：城池，指护城河。［4］效：
献出。

【译文】滕文公问道："滕国是一个小国，夹
在齐国和楚国之间。是侍奉齐国呢，还是侍
奉楚国呢？"

　　孟子回答说："这种谋略不是我所能达
到的。不得已非要我说的话，那么只有一个
办法：挖深护城河，筑牢城墙，并与百姓共
同守护它，即使献出生命，百姓也不离开。
如果这样，此法便可以保家卫国了。"

【解读】孟子在本章中回答了一个关乎生死存
亡的大问题：在大国的夹缝中，一个小国如
何求得生存，如何自我保全。任何一个国家、
一个民族面临生存危机，都是一个极端严峻
的问题，处理不好稍有不慎就会有倾覆之危、
灭顶之灾，面对这样的危机，小国尤甚。而

滕国就是一个这样弱小的国家，处于北方富庶的齐国和南方广袤的楚国两个强大的国家之间，况且在那个无义战的战国中后期，天下风云激荡，大国纵横捭阖，兼并战争愈演愈烈。

滕国如何自处，考验着国君滕文公的智慧，滕国依附任何一方，都无异于自掘坟墓。孟子面对这样棘手的问题睿智地指出，做好自己的事情才是唯一的出路。如何做好自己的事情呢？朱熹说："国君死社稷，故致死以守国。至于民亦为之死守而不去，则非有以深得其心者不能也。此章言有国者当守义而爱民，不可侥幸而苟免。"（朱熹《四书章句集注》）孟子的意思是要做好防卫，国君与百姓上下一心，休戚与共；朱熹更进一步指出，要想让百姓与国君同心同德共存亡，那就要求国君行仁义之政，爱护百姓，民心可用，才能众志成城。

2.14

滕文公问曰：“齐人将筑薛[1]，吾甚恐，如之何则可？”

孟子对曰：“昔者大王居邠[2]，狄人侵之，去之岐山之下居焉。非择而取之，不得已也。苟为善，后世子孙必有王者矣。君子创业垂统，为可继也。若夫成功，则天也。君如彼何哉？强为善而已矣。”

The duke Wen of Teng asked Mencius, saying, "The people of Qi are going to fortify Xue. The movement occasions me great alarm. What is the proper course for me to take in the case?"

Mencius replied, "Formerly, when king Tai dwelt in Bin, the barbarians of the north were continually making incursions upon it. He therefore left it, went to the foot of mount Qi, and there took up his residence. He did not take that situation, as having selected it. It was a matter of necessity with him. If you do good, among your descendants, in after generations, there shall be one who will attain to the royal dignity. A prince lays the foundation of the inheritance, and hands down the beginning which he has made, doing what may be continued by his successors. As to the accomplishment of the great result, that is with Heaven. What is that Qi to you, O prince? Be strong to do good. That is all your business."

【注释】［1］薛：国名，其地在今山东滕州东南，战国初期为齐所灭，后成为齐权臣田婴、田文的封邑。［2］邠（bīn）：地名，在今陕西郴县。

【译文】滕文公问："齐国将要修筑薛城，我十分害怕，怎么办才好呢？"

孟子回答："从前周太王古公亶甫居住在

邠地，狄人侵犯那里，他便迁到岐山下居住。他并不愿意选择那里居住，不得已罢了。如果实施善政，后代子孙必会有可以称王天下的。君子创立基业，代代相传，是为了可以被继承下去。至于能否成功，就要看天意了。您对齐国能怎么样呢？只有努力推行善政罢了。"

【解读】滕文公面对强齐压境修筑薛城，乱了方寸，惶恐失措，向孟子请教应对之策。孟子以周太王避狄人侵袭迁居到岐山之下为例，劝说滕文公勉力推行仁政来保境安民。周太王避让强敌，力行仁善，后世子孙周文王、周武王反而拥有了天下。孟子的意思是，面对强敌，为子孙基业考虑，先避敌锋芒，然后努力施行仁政。至于最终能否成功，一切都只能取决于天意了。朱熹说："能为善，则如大王虽失其地，而其后世遂有天下，乃天理也。然君子造基业于前，而垂统绪于后，但能不失其正，令后世可继续而行耳。若夫

成功，则岂可必乎？彼，齐也。君之力既无如之何，则但强于为善，使其可继而俟命于天耳。"（朱熹《四书章句集注》）

2.15

　　滕文公问曰:"滕,小国也。竭力以事大国,则不得免焉。如之何则可?"

　　孟子对曰:"昔者大王居邠,狄人侵之。事之以皮币[1],不得免焉;事之以犬马,不得免焉;事之以珠玉,不得免焉。乃属其耆老[2]而告之曰:'狄人之所欲者,吾土地也。吾闻之也:君子不以其所以养人者害人。二三子何患乎无君?我将去之。'去邠,逾梁山,邑于岐山之下居焉。邠人曰:'仁人也,不可失也。'从之者如归市。或曰:'世守也,非身之所能为也。效死勿去。'君请择于斯二者。"

The duke Wen of Teng asked Mencius, saying, "Teng is a small state. Though I do my utmost to serve those large kingdoms on either side of it, we cannot escape suffering from them. What course shall I take that we may do so?"

Mencius replied, "Formerly, when king Tai dwelt in Bin, the barbarians of the north were constantly making incursions upon it. He served them with skins and silks, and still he suffered from them. He served them with dogs and horses, and still he suffered from them. He served them with pearls and gems, and still he suffered from them. Seeing this, he assembled the old men, and announced to them, saying, 'What the barbarians want is my territory. I have heard this—that a ruler does not injure his people with that wherewith he nourishes them. My children, why should you be troubled about having no prince? I will leave this.' Accordingly, he left Bin, crossed the mountain Liang, built a town at the foot of mount Qi, and dwelt there. The people of Pin said, 'He is a benevolent man. We must not lose him.' Those who followed him looked like crowds hastening to market. On the other hand, some say, 'The kingdom is a thing to be kept from generation to generation. One individual cannot undertake to dispose of it in his own person. Let him be prepared to die for it. Let him not quit it.' I ask you, prince, to make your election between these two courses."

【注释】［1］皮币：动物毛皮和丝绸布帛之类的礼品。［2］耆老：老年人。

【译文】滕文公问："滕国是个小国，竭力去侍奉大国，却无法免于亡国的危险，怎么办才好呢？"

孟子回答："从前，周太王居住在邠地，狄人侵犯那里。他拿兽皮丝绸送给狄人，不能免遭侵犯；拿宝马名犬送给狄人，不能免遭侵犯；拿珠宝玉器送给狄人，不能免遭侵犯。于是召集邠地的老年人，对他们说：'狄人想要的，是我们的土地。我听说过这样的

话：君子不拿用来供养人的东西害人。你们
何必担心没有君主？我将要离开这个地方。'
于是离开邠地，越过梁山，在岐山下建城邑
定居下来。邠地的人说：'是个仁人啊，不
能失去他啊。'追随他的人像赶集市一样多。
有人说：'土地是必须世代守护的，不能擅
自丢弃，宁愿死也不能离开。'请您在这两
者中选择吧。"

【解读】本章中孟子与滕文公的对话，依然是
探讨滕国作为一个小国，在列强环伺之下如
何生存的问题。孟子与滕文公的三次对话，
基本围绕同一个问题，孟子给出的对策却不
尽相同，这颇为耐人寻味。面对周边强国环
伺的严峻形势，滕文公焦虑不安，孟子也表
现出力有未逮的无奈。滕文公的第三次请教，
孟子更是给出了一个选择式的答案，他告诉
滕君，要么仿效周太王，面对强大的狄人的
侵扰，迁移到他处而居；要么是对于先祖传

下的基业誓死守卫，与民效死守之。程氏门人杨时对此评述说："孟子之于文公，始告之以效死而已，礼之正也。至其甚恐，则以大王之事告之，非得已也。然无大王之德而去，则民或不从而遂至于亡，则又不若效死之为愈。故又请择于斯二者。"（朱熹《四书章句集注》）其实，孟子还是希望滕文公施行仁政，从而达到保国安民的目的。因为选择如周太王那样迁居，必须如太王那样施行仁政，冀后世能"王天下"；选择死守，也必须推行仁政，爱护百姓，百姓方能与君王同生共死。所以，无论滕文公做何选择，孟子的主张都是非常明确的，那就是勉力为善，施行仁政。

2.16

鲁平公[1]将出。嬖人[2]臧仓者请曰："他日君出,则必命有司所之。今乘舆已驾矣,有司未知所之。敢请。"

公曰："将见孟子。"

曰："何哉?君所为轻身以先于匹夫者,以为贤乎?礼义由贤者出,而孟子之后丧逾前丧[3]。君无见焉!"

公曰："诺。"

乐正子入见,曰："君奚为不见孟轲也?"

曰："或告寡人曰'孟子之后丧逾前丧',是以不往见也。"

曰："何哉君所谓逾者?前以士,后以大夫;前以三鼎,而后以五鼎与?"

曰："否。谓棺椁衣衾之美也。"

曰："非所谓逾也,贫富不同也。"

乐正子见孟子,曰："克[4]告于君,君为来见也。嬖人有臧仓者沮[5]君,君是以不果来也。”

曰：“行或使之，止或尼^[6]之。行止，非人所能也。吾之不遇鲁侯，天也。臧氏之子焉能使予不遇哉？”

The duke Ping of Lu was about to leave his palace, when his favourite, one Zang Cang, made a request to him, saying, "On other days, when you have gone out, you have given instructions to the officers as to where you were going. But now, the horses have been put to the carriage, and the officers do not yet know where you are going. I venture to ask."

The duke said, "I am going to see the scholar Meng."

"How is this?" said the other. "That you demean yourself, prince, in paying the honour of the first visit to a common man, is, I suppose, because you think that he is a man of talents and virtue. By such men the rules of ceremonial proprieties and right are observed.

But on the occasion of this Meng's second mourning, his observances exceeded those of the former. Do not go to see him, my prince."

The duke said, "I will not."

The officer Yue Zheng entered the court, and had an audience. He said, "Prince, why have you not gone to see Meng Ke?"

The duke said, "One told me that, on the occasion of the scholar Meng's second mourning, his observances exceeded those of the former. It is on that account that I have not gone to see him."

"How is this!" answered Yue Zheng. "By what you call 'exceeding,' you mean, I suppose, that, on the first occasion, he used the rites appropriate to a scholar, and, on the second, those appropriate to a great officer; that he first used three tripods, and afterwards five tripods."

The duke said, "No. I refer to the greater excellence of the coffin, the shell, the grave-clothes, and the shroud."

Yue Zheng said, "That cannot be called 'exceeding.' That was the difference between being poor and being rich."

After this, Yue Zheng saw Mencius, and said to him, "I told the prince about you, and he was consequently coming to see you, when one of his favourites, named Zang Cang, stopped him, and therefore he did not come according to his purpose."

Mencius said, "A man's advancement is effected, it may be, by others, and the stopping him is, it may be, from the efforts of others. But to advance a man or to stop his advance is really beyond the power of other men. My not finding in the prince of Lu a ruler who would confide in me, and put my counsels into practice, is from Heaven. How could that scion of the Zang family cause me not to find the ruler that would suit me?"

【注释】[1]鲁平公：鲁国国君，景公的儿子，名姬叔，谥号平。[2]嬖人：被宠幸的人，此处指亲信的小臣。[3]后丧逾前丧：后丧指其母丧，前丧指其父丧。此谓母丧之礼超过了父丧。[4]克：乐正子之名。[5]沮（jǔ）：阻止。[6]尼（nǐ）：阻止。

【译文】鲁平公准备外出，他亲近的小臣臧仓请示说："平日您外出，一定要告诉管事的人您去哪儿。现在车马都准备好了，管事的人还不知道您要到哪儿去，胆敢请示一下。"

鲁平公说："要去拜访孟子。"

（臧仓）说："为什么呢？您轻视自己的身份先去拜访一个普通人，以为他是一个贤人吗？礼义应该是由贤者做出表率的，而孟子办他母亲的丧事比他从前办父亲的丧事隆重，您还是不要去见他！"

鲁平公说："好吧。"

乐正子入宫拜见鲁平公，问道："您为

什么不去见孟轲呀？"

（鲁平公）说："有人告诉我'孟子办母亲的丧事超过父亲的丧事'，所以我不去见他。"

（乐正子）说："您所说的超过是指什么呢？是指前以士礼为父亲办丧事，后以大夫礼为母亲办丧事；还是指前以三鼎之礼为父亲办丧事，后以五鼎之礼为母亲办丧事？"

（鲁平公）说："不是的。是说棺材及寿衣的华美。"

（乐正子）说："这不能叫'超过'，是前后贫富不同的缘故。"

乐正子拜见孟子，说："我把您推荐给了鲁君，鲁君打算来见您。有一个叫臧仓的宠臣阻止了他，所以他最终没有来。"

（孟子）说："他来或许有人让他来，他不来或许有人阻止他来。来与不来，不是人为所决定的。我没能见到鲁君，是天意啊。姓臧的家伙怎么能让我见不到鲁君呢？"

《孟子》插圖

魯平公將出，嬖人臧倉者請曰：他日君出則必
命有司所之；今乘輿已駕矣，有司未知所之，敢請。
公曰將見孟子。曰何哉，君所為輕身以先於匹
夫者以為賢乎，禮義由賢者出，而孟子之後
喪踰前喪，君無見焉。公曰諾。歲次庚子之春永生畫并

亲贤臣，远小人　徐永生　绘

【解读】本章记述的是鲁平公与孟子之间君臣不遇的一桩往事。战国时期，鲁国已日渐式微，江河日下。鲁平公践位之后，礼贤下士，图谋振兴，欲往拜孟子，临行时却被一个小臣臧仓的一番话阻止了。臧仓说，孟子行事不合礼仪，为母亲办丧事的规格高于先去世的父亲。事实上，这只是托词而已，欲加之罪，何患无辞！孟子的身份先后发生了变化，政治身份和社会地位与父亲去世时已大不同。按照儒家崇尚的周礼规定，孟子并未僭越周礼。孟子与鲁君不得会见，在孟子看来，如果鲁平公是一位贤明国君，就不会因小人臧仓的一番话而改变主意。国君昏庸，宠信小人，国家运势的衰落是必然的，不是他人所能左右的，冥冥之中似有天意。正如朱熹所言："此章言圣贤之出处，关时运之盛衰，乃天命之所为，非人力之可及。"（朱熹《四书章句集注》）可见亲贤臣，远小人对于国君治理国家多么重要！

公孙丑上

Gong Sun Chou 1

3.1

公孙丑[1]问曰："夫子当路于齐[2]，管仲、晏子之功，可复许[3]乎？"

孟子曰："子诚齐人也，知管仲、晏子而已矣。或问乎曾西[4]曰：'吾子与子路孰贤？'曾西蹵然[5]曰：'吾先子[6]之所畏也。'曰：'然则吾子与管仲孰贤？'曾西艴然[7]不悦，曰：'尔何曾[8]比予于管仲？管仲得君，如彼其专也；行乎国政，如彼其久也；功烈，如彼其卑也。尔何曾比予于是？'"

曰："管仲，曾西之所不为也，而子为[9]我愿之乎？"

曰："管仲以其君霸，晏子以其君显。管仲、晏子犹不足为与？"

曰："以齐王，由[10]反手也。"

曰："若是，则弟子之惑滋甚。且以文王之德，百年而后崩，犹未洽[11]于天下；武王、周公继之，然后大行。今言王若易然，则文王不足法与？"

曰："文王何可当也？由汤至于武丁，贤圣之君六七作。天下归殷久矣，久则难变也。武丁朝诸侯有天下，犹运之掌也。纣之去武丁未久也，其故家遗俗，流风善政，犹有存者；又有微子、微仲、王子比干、箕子、胶鬲皆贤人也，相与辅相[12]之，故久而后失之也。尺地莫非其有也，一民莫非其臣也，然而文王犹方百里起，是以难也。齐人有言曰：'虽有智慧，不如乘势；虽有镃基[13]，不如待时。'今时则易然也。夏后、殷、周之盛，地未有过千里者也，而齐有其地矣；鸡鸣狗吠相闻，而达乎四境，而齐有其民矣。地不改辟矣，民不改聚矣，行仁政而王，莫之能御也。且王者之不作，未有疏于此时者也；民之憔悴[14]于虐政，未有甚于此时者也。饥者易为食，渴者易为饮。孔子曰：'德之流行，速于置邮[15]而传命。'当今之时，万乘之国行仁政，民之悦之，犹解倒悬也。故事半古之人，功必倍之，惟此时为然。"

Gongsun Chou asked Mencius, saying, "Master, if you were to obtain the ordering of the government in Qi, could you promise yourself to accomplish anew such results as those realized by Guan Zhong and Yan?"

Mencius said, "You are indeed a true man of Qi. You know about Guan Zhong and Yan, and nothing more. Some one asked Zeng Xi, saying, 'Sir, to which do you give the superiority, to yourself or to Zilu?' Zeng Xi looked uneasy, and said, 'He was an object of veneration to my grandfather.' 'Then,' pursued the other, 'do you give the superiority to yourself or to Guan Zhong?' Zeng Xi, flushed with anger and displeased, said, 'How dare you compare me with Guan Zhong? Considering how entirely Guan Zhong possessed the confidence of his prince, how long he enjoyed the direction of the government of the state, and how low, after all, was what he accomplished—how is it that you liken me to him?' Thus."

Concluded Mencius, "Zeng Xi would not play Guan Zhong, and is it what you desire for me that I should do so?"

Gong Sun Chou said, "Guan Zhong raised his prince to be the leader of all the other princes, and Yan made his prince illustrious, and do you still think it would not be enough for you to do what they did?"

Mencius answered, "To raise Qi to the royal dignity would be as easy as it is to turn round the hand."

"So!" returned the other. "The perplexity of your disciple is hereby very much increased. There was king Wen, moreover, with all the virtue which belonged to him; and who did not die till he had reached a hundred years—and still his influence had not penetrated throughout the kingdom. It required king Wu and the duke of Zhou to continue his course, before that influence greatly prevailed. Now you say that the royal dignity might be so easily obtained: —is king Wen then not a sufficient object for imitation?"

Mencius said, "How can king Wen be matched? From Tang to Wu Ding there had appeared six or seven worthy and sage sovereigns. The kingdom had been attached to Yin for a long time, and this length of time made a change difficult. Wu Ding had all the princes coming to his court, and possessed the kingdom as if it had been a thing which he moved round in his palm. Then, Zhou was removed from Wu Ding by no great interval of time. There were still remaining some of the ancient families and of the old manners, of the influence also which had emanated from the earlier sovereigns, and of their good government. Moreover, there were the viscount of Wei and his second son, their Royal Highnesses Bi Gan and the viscount of Qi, and Jiao Ge, all men of ability and virtue, who gave their joint assistance to Zhou in his government. In consequence of these things, it took a long time for him to lose the throne. There was not a foot of ground which he did not possess. There was not one of all the people who was not his subject. So it was on his side, and king Wen at his beginning had only a territory of one hundred square *li*. On all these accounts, it was difficult for him immediately to attain to the royal dignity. The people of Qi have a saying—'A man may have wisdom and discernment, but that is not like embracing the favourable opportunity. A man may have instruments of husbandry, but that is not like waiting for the farming seasons.' The present time is one in which the royal dignity may be easily attained. In the flourishing periods of the Xia, Yin, and Zhou dynasties, the royal domain did not exceed a thousand *li*, and Qi embraces so much territory. Cocks crow and dogs bark to one another, all the way to the four borders of the State—so Qi possesses the people. No change is needed for the enlarging of its territory; no change is needed for the collecting of a population. If its ruler will put in practice a benevolent government, no power will be able to prevent his becoming sovereign. Moreover, never was there a time farther removed than the present from the rise of a true sovereign: never was there a time when the sufferings of the people from tyrannical government were more intense than the present. The hungry readily partake of any food, and the thirsty of any drink. Confucius said, 'The flowing progress of virtue is more rapid than the transmission of royal orders by stages and couriers.' At the present time, in a country of ten thousand chariots, let benevolent government be put in practice, and the people will be delighted with it, as if they were relieved from hanging by the heels. With half the merit of the ancients, double their achievements is sure to be realized. It is only at this time that such could be the case."

【注释】[1] 公孙丑：孟子弟子。[2] 夫子：指孟子。当路：当政。[3] 许：期望，这里作"兴起"解。[4] 曾西：字子照，曾参之孙，曾元之子。[5] 蹴（cù）然：不安的样子。[6] 先子：古人用以称其已逝世的长辈，这里指曾西的亡祖父曾参。[7] 艴（fú）然：生气的样子。[8] 何曾：为何，何故。曾：竟。[9] 为：认为。[10] 由：通"犹"，好像。[11] 洽：统一。[12] 辅相：辅助。[13] 镃（zī）基：农具，锄头之类。[14] 憔悴：困顿。[15] 置邮：置和邮都是名词，相当于后代的驿站。

【译文】公孙丑问道："如果您在齐国当政，像管仲、晏子那样的功业，可以再度兴起吗？"

孟子说："你真是个齐国人啊，只知道管仲、晏婴。曾经有人问曾西：'您和子路比较谁更贤能？'曾西不安地说：'子路是我先人所敬畏的人啊。'那人又问：'那么您和管仲谁更贤能？'曾西很生气，说：'你为何把我和管仲相比呢？管仲得到君主独有的信任是那样专一，领国政那样久，功绩却是如此卑小，你为何拿他来和我相比呢？'"

（孟子接着）说："管仲这种人，连曾西都不愿做，你认为我愿意效法他吗？"

（公孙丑）说："管仲辅佐齐桓公称霸，晏子辅佐齐景公闻名。难道管仲、晏婴这样的人，还不值得效法吗？"

（孟子）说："凭借齐国来称霸天下，就像把手掌反过来一样简单。"

（公孙丑）说："如果这样的话，弟子的疑惑就更多了。况且以周文王那样的仁德，将近活了一百年，还没能统一天下。周武王、周公继承他的事业，然后才王道大行。现在您把用王道统一天下说得很容易的样子，那么，连周文王都不值得效法了吗？"

（孟子）说："怎么可以和周文王相比呢？由商汤到武丁，贤明的君主有六七个，天下人归顺殷朝很久了，时间越长越难以改变。武丁使诸侯们来朝，统治天下就像在自己的手掌心里运转物件一样容易。纣王离武丁时间并不长，勋臣旧戚之家风遗俗、良风善令都还有遗存；又有微子、微仲、王子比干、箕子、胶鬲等一批贤臣共同辅佐，所以能统治很久后才失去政权。当时，每一尺土地，无不归纣王所有，每一个百姓，无不是纣王的臣民；然而文王还能仅靠方圆百里的土地兴起，所以是非常困难的。齐国人有句话说：'即使有智慧，不如趁形势；即使有锄头，不如等农时。'现在是时候了，所以说很容易。夏、商、周三代兴盛的时候，国土没有超过方圆千里的，而现在的齐国有了这么大的国土；鸡鸣狗叫的声音，彼此都能听到，一直传到四方边境，这说明齐国拥有众多的百姓。土地不需要重新开辟，民众不需要重新聚集，只要施行仁政，就能统一天下，没有什么能够阻挡。况且，圣贤君王不出现，没有比这一时期更稀少了；百姓困顿于暴虐之政，比任何时候都严重。饥饿的人可以很容易让他吃饱，口渴的人可以很容易让他喝足。孔子说：'德政的流传，快于驿站传递政令。'当今这个时候，拥有万辆兵车的大国施行仁政，老百姓高兴得就像被倒吊着的人得到解救一样。所以，只要用上古人做事一半的功夫，就能得到比古人多一倍的功业，只有这个时候才能办到。"

【解读】管仲曾经辅助齐桓公"尊王攘夷""九合诸侯"，成为一代霸主；晏婴曾辅佐齐景公扬名诸侯。公孙丑又是齐国人，必定非常熟悉二人的事迹功业，对此二人也是充满敬意，故以此来期许孟子。孟子却对此不屑一顾，认为管仲不值得效仿，并以曾西事例加以说明。同时还审时度势地认为凭齐国的条件与基础，称霸天下易如反掌。孟子的壮志让公孙丑更加疑惑："管仲、晏子犹不足为与"，连周文王都不能实现的目标，您却说得如此轻而易举？

孟子结合商周易代时的形势，总结出了周文王难以推行"王道"的两大原因：一方面是因为殷商有武丁以来良好的统治基础，有诸多贤臣的辅佐，所以即便暴君在位，也是短时间难以动摇的；另一方面，与殷商相比，周文王的土地、百姓太少，所以想要兴起也不是容易的事情。然而齐国不同，不仅有足够的土地和民众（地利），而且当时已少有圣王在世，百姓久被暴政残虐（天时），只要齐国此时肯施行仁政（人和），那么便可得到事半功倍的效果，所以孟子才有信心对公孙丑说出"惟此时为然"。当然，在当时的历史背景下，孟子的这一主张显得过于理想化，但是其言语间所流露出来的对于"仁政"的执着与坚守，确实让人佩服！

孟子与公孙丑席地而论　梁文博　绘

3.2

公孙丑问曰：“夫子加^[1]齐之卿相，得
行道焉，虽由此霸王不异^[2]矣。如此，则动
心否乎？”

孟子曰：“否。我四十不动心。”

曰：“若是，则夫子过孟贲^[3]远矣。”

曰：“是不难，告子^[4]先我不动心。”

曰：“不动心有道乎？”

曰：“有。北宫黝^[5]之养勇也，不肤挠^[6]，
不目逃^[7]，思以一豪挫于人，若挞^[8]之于市朝。
不受于褐宽博^[9]，亦不受于万乘之君。视刺
万乘之君，若刺褐夫。无严^[10]诸侯。恶声至，
必反之。孟施舍之所养勇也，曰：‘视不胜
犹胜也。量敌而后进，虑胜而后会，是畏三
军者也。舍岂能为必胜哉？能无惧而已矣。’
孟施舍似曾子，北宫黝似子夏。夫二子之勇，
未知其孰贤，然而孟施舍守约^[11]也。昔者曾
子谓子襄^[12]曰：‘子好勇乎？吾尝闻大勇于

夫子矣：自反而不缩[13]，虽褐宽博，吾不惴焉；自反而缩，虽千万人，吾往矣。'孟施舍之守气，又不如曾子之守约也。"

曰："敢问夫子之不动心，与告子之不动心，可得闻与？"

"告子曰：'不得于言，勿求于心；不得于心，勿求于气。'不得于心，勿求于气，可；不得于言，勿求于心，不可。夫志，气之帅也；气，体之充也。夫志至焉，气次焉。故曰：'持其志，无暴其气。'"

"既曰'志至焉，气次焉'，又曰'持其志无暴其气'者，何也？"

曰："志壹[14]则动气，气壹则动志也。今夫蹶[15]者趋者，是气也，而反动其心。"

"敢问夫子恶乎长？"

曰："我知言，我善养吾浩然之气。"

"敢问何谓浩然之气？"

曰："难言也。其为气也，至大至刚，以直养而无害，则塞于天地之间。其为气也，配义与道；无是，馁也。是集义所生者，非义袭而取之也。行有不慊[16]于心，则馁矣。我故曰，告子未尝知义，以其外之也。必有事焉而勿正[17]，心勿忘，勿助长也。无若宋人然：宋人有闵其苗之不长而揠之者，芒芒然归。谓其人曰：'今日病矣，予助苗长矣。'其子趋而往视之，苗则槁矣。天下之不助苗长者寡矣。以为无益而舍之者，不耘苗者也；助之长者，揠苗者也。非徒无益，而又害之。"

"何谓知言？"

曰："诐[18]辞知其所蔽，淫辞知其所陷，邪辞知其所离，遁辞知其所穷。生于其心，害于其政；发于其政，害于其事。圣人复起，必从吾言矣。"

"宰我、子贡善为说辞，冉牛、闵子、颜渊善言德行。孔子兼之，曰：'我于辞命则不能也。'然则夫子既圣矣乎？"

曰："恶！是何言也？昔者子贡问于孔子曰：'夫子圣矣乎？'孔子曰：'圣则吾不能，

我学不厌而教不倦也。'子贡曰:'学不厌,智也;教不倦,仁也。仁且智,夫子既圣矣!'夫圣,孔子不居,是何言也?"

"昔者窃闻之:子夏、子游、子张皆有圣人之一体,冉牛、闵子、颜渊则具体而微。敢问所安。"

曰:"姑舍是。"

曰:"伯夷、伊尹何如?"

曰:"不同道。非其君不事,非其民不使;治则进,乱则退,伯夷也。何事非君,何使非民;治亦进,乱亦进,伊尹也。可以仕则仕,可以止则止,可以久则久,可以速则速,孔子也。皆古圣人也,吾未能有行焉;乃所愿,则学孔子也。"

"伯夷、伊尹于孔子,若是班[19]乎?"

曰:"否。自有生民以来,未有孔子也。"

曰:"然则有同与?"

曰:"有。得百里之地而君之,皆能以朝诸侯,有天下。行一不义,杀一不辜而得天下，皆不为也。是则同。"

日："敢问其所以异？"

日："宰我、子贡、有若，智足以知圣人。污[20]，不至阿其所好。宰我曰：'以予观于夫子，贤于尧、舜远矣。'子贡曰：'见其礼而知其政，闻其乐而知其德，由百世之后，等百世之王，莫之能违也。自生民以来，未有夫子也。'有若曰：'岂惟民哉？麒麟之于走兽，凤凰之于飞鸟，太山之于丘垤[21]，河海之于行潦[22]，类也。圣人之于民，亦类也。出于其类，拔乎其萃，自生民以来，未有盛于孔子也。'"

Gongsun Chou asked Mencius, saying, "Master, if you were to be appointed a high noble and the prime minister of Qi, so as to be able to carry your principles into practice, though you should thereupon raise the ruler to the headship of all the other princes, or even to the royal dignity, it would not be to be wondered at. In such a position would your mind be perturbed or not?"

Mencius replied, "No. At forty, I attained to an unperturbed mind."

Chou said, "Since it is so with you, my Master, you are far beyond Meng Ben."

"The mere attainment," said Mencius, "is not difficult. The scholar Gao had attained to an unperturbed mind at an earlier period of life than I did."

Chou asked, "Is there any way to an unperturbed mind?"

The answer was, "Yes. Beigong You had this way of nourishing his valour: He did not flinch from any strokes at his body. He did not turn his eyes aside from any thrusts at them. He considered that the slightest push from any one was the same as if he were beaten before the crowds in the market-place, and that what he would not receive from a common man in his loose large garments of hair, neither should he receive from a prince of ten thousand chariots. He viewed stabbing a prince of ten thousand chariots just as stabbing a fellow dressed in cloth of hair. He feared not any of all the princes. A bad word addressed to him be always returned. Meng Shishe had this way of nourishing his valour: He said, 'I look upon not conquering and conquering in the same way. To measure the enemy and then advance; to calculate the chances of victory and then engage: —this is to stand in awe of the opposing force. How can I make certain of conquering? I can only rise superior to all fear.' Meng Shishe resembled the philosopher Zeng. Beigong You resembled Zixia. I do not know to the valour of which of the two the superiority should be ascribed, but yet Meng Shishe attended to what was of the greater importance. Formerly, the philosopher Zeng said to Zixiang, 'Do you love valour? I heard an account of great valour from the Master. It speaks thus: If, on self-examination, I find that I am not upright, shall I not be in fear even of a poor man in his loose garments of hair-cloth? If, on self-examination, I find that I am upright, I will go forward against thousands and tens of thousands.' Yet, what Meng Shishe maintained, being merely his physical energy, was after all inferior to what the philosopher Zeng maintained, which was indeed of the most importance."

Gongsun Chou said, "May I venture to ask an explanation from you, Master, of how you maintain an unperturbed mind, and how the philosopher Gao does the same?"

Mencius answered, "Gao says, 'What is not attained in words is not to be sought for in the mind; what produces dissatisfaction in the mind, is not to be helped by passion-effort.' This last, when there is unrest in the mind, not to seek for relief from passion-effort, may be conceded. But not to seek in the mind for what is not attained in words cannot be conceded. The will is the leader of the passion-nature. The passion-nature pervades and animates the body. The will is first and chief, and the passion-nature is subordinate to it. Therefore I say, Maintain firm the will, and do no violence to the passion-nature."

Chou observed, "Since you say 'The will is chief, and the passion-nature is subordinate,' how do you also say, 'Maintain firm the will, and do no violence to the passion-nature?'"

Mencius replied, "When it is the will alone which is active, it moves the passion-nature. When it is the passion-nature alone which is active, it moves the will. For instance now, in the case of a man falling or running, that is from the passion-nature, and yet it moves the mind."

"I venture to ask," said Chou again, "wherein

you, Master, surpass Gao."

Mencius told him, "I understand words. I am skilful in nourishing my vast, flowing passion-nature."

Chou pursued, "I venture to ask what you mean by your vast, flowing passion-nature!"

The reply was, "It is difficult to describe it. This is the passion-nature: — It is exceedingly great, and exceedingly strong. Being nourished by rectitude, and sustaining no injury, it fills up all between heaven and earth. This is the passion-nature: — It is the mate and assistant of righteousness and reason. Without it, man is in a state of starvation. It is produced by the accumulation of righteous deeds; it is not to be obtained by incidental acts of righteousness. If the mind does not feel complacency in the conduct, the nature becomes starved. I therefore said, 'Gao has never understood righteousness, because he makes it something external.' There must be the constant practice of this righteousness, but without the object of thereby nourishing the passion-nature. Let not the mind forget its work, but let there be no assisting the growth of that nature. Let us not be like the man of Song. There was a man of Song, who was grieved that his growing corn was not longer, and so he pulled it up. Having done this, he returned home, looking very stupid, and said to his people, 'I am tired today. I have been helping the corn to grow long.' His son ran to look at it, and found the corn all withered. There are few in the world, who do not deal with their passion-nature, as if they were assisting the corn to grow long. Some indeed consider it of no benefit to them, and let it alone: — they do not weed their corn. They who assist it to grow long pull out their corn. What they do is not only of no benefit to the nature, but it also injures it."

Gongsun Chou further asked, "What do you mean by saying that you understand whatever words you hear?"

Mencius replied, "When words are one-sided, I know how the mind of the speaker is clouded over. When words are extravagant, I know how the mind is fallen and sunk. When words are all-depraved, I know how the mind has departed from principle. When words are evasive, I know how the mind is at its wit's end. These evils growing in the mind, do injury to government, and, displayed in the government, are hurtful to the conduct of affairs. When a sage shall again arise, he will certainly follow my words."

On this Chou observed, "Zai Wo and Zigong were skilful in speaking. Ran Niu, the disciple Min, and Yan Yuan, while their words were good, were distinguished for their virtuous conduct. Confucius united the qualities of the disciples in himself, but still he said, 'In the matter of speeches, I am not competent.' —Then, Master, have you attained to be a sage?"

Mencius said, "Oh! what words are these? Formerly Zigong asked Confucius, saying, 'Master, are you a sage?' Confucius answered him, 'A sage is what l cannot rise to. I learn without satiety, and teach without being tired.' Zigong said, 'You learn without satiety—that shows your wisdom. You teach without being tired—that shows your benevolence. Benevolent and wise—Master, you ARE a sage.' Now, since Confucius would not allow himself to be regarded as a sage, what words were those?"

Chou said, "Formerly, I once heard this: Zi -xia, Ziyou, and Zizhang had each one member of the sage. Ran Niu, the disciple Min, and Yan Yuan had all the members, but in small proportions. I venture to ask, With which of these are you pleased to rank yourself?"

Mencius replied, "Let us drop speaking about these, if you please."

Chou then asked, "What do you say of Boyi and Yiyin?"

"Their ways were different from mine," said Mencius. "Not to serve a prince whom he did not esteem, nor command a people whom he did not approve; in a time of good government to take office, and on the occurrence of confusion to retire — this was the way of Boyi. To say 'Whom may I not serve? My serving him makes him my ruler. What people may I not command? My commanding them makes them my people.' In a time of good government to take office, and when disorder prevailed, also to take office — that was the way of Yiyin. When it was proper to go into office, then to go into it; when it was proper to keep retired from office, then to keep retired from it; when it was proper to continue in it long, then to continue in it long — when it was proper to withdraw from it quickly, then to withdraw quickly — that was the way of Confucius. These were all sages of antiquity, and I have not attained to do what they did. But what I wish to do is to learn to be like Confucius."

Chou said, "Comparing Boyi and Yiyin with Confucius, are they to be placed in the same rank?"

Mencius replied, "No. Since there were living men until now, there never was another Confucius."

Chou said, "Then, did they have any points of agreement with him?"

The reply was, "Yes. If they had been sovereigns over a hundred *li* of territory, they would, all of them, have brought all the princes to attend in their court, and have obtained the throne. And none of them, in order to obtain the throne, would have committed one act of unrighteousness, or put to death one innocent person. In those things they agreed with him."

Chou said, "I venture to ask wherein he differed from them."

Mencius replied, "Zai Wo, Zigong, and You Ruo had wisdom sufficient to know the sage. Even had they been ranking themselves low, they would not have demeaned themselves to flatter their favourite. Now, Zai Wo said, 'According to my view of our Master, he was far superior to Yao and Shun.' Zigong said, 'By viewing the ceremonial ordinances of a prince, we know the character of his government. By hearing his music, we know the character of his virtue. After the lapse of a hundred ages I can arrange, according to their merits, the kings of a hundred ages—not one of them can escape me. From the birth of mankind till now, there has never been another like our Master.' You Ruo said, 'Is it only among men that it is so? There is the Qi-lin among quadrupeds, the Fenghuang among birds, the Tai mountain among mounds and anthills, and rivers and seas among rain-pools. Though different in degree, they are the same in kind. So the sages among mankind are also the same in kind. But they stand out from their fellows, and rise above the level, and from the birth of mankind till now, there never has been one so complete as Confucius.'"

【注释】［1］加：居，担任。［2］不异：不认为奇怪。［3］孟贲：古代勇士。［4］告子：孟子同时期人，姓告名不害，兼学儒墨之道。《孟子》中有《告子》篇。［5］北宫黝：复姓北宫，名黝，齐国人。［6］肤挠：肌肤被刺而挠屈，犹言示弱，屈服。［7］目逃：眼睛受刺而躲开。［8］挞：鞭打。［9］褐宽博：穿宽大粗布衣的人。褐：粗布衣，贫贱者所服。［10］严：畏惧。［11］约（yāo）：通"要"，纲要，要领。［12］子襄：曾子弟子。［13］缩：朱熹《孟子集注》解"直也"。应当"义"解。［14］壹：专一。［15］蹶（jué）：跌倒。［16］慊（qiè）：快心，满意。［17］正：止。［18］诐（bì）：偏颇，偏执。［19］班：等同，并列。

[20]污：污下，不高洁。[21]丘垤（dié）：小山丘，小土堆。[22]行潦（lǎo）：水沟。

【译文】 公孙丑问孟子说："如果您担任齐国的国相，可以施行仁道，即使由此而成就霸业和王道也不认为奇怪。像这样的话，您是否会动心呢？"

孟子说："不会。我四十岁起就不会动心了。"

（公孙丑）说："如果是这样，那么您远超过孟贲了。"

（孟子）答道："这并不难，告子在我之前就不动心了。"

（公孙丑）问道："不动心有方法吗？"

（孟子）说："有。北宫黝这样来培养勇气，肌肤被刺痛时不屈服，眼睛被刺激时不逃避，但他认为受了一点他人侮辱的时候，就像在大庭广众下被人鞭打一样。既不愿受制于布衣百姓的羞辱，也不愿受制于大国君

王的羞辱。把刺杀大国国君看作刺杀布衣百
姓一样，不惧怕诸侯。听了不好的言论，一
定要反击。孟施舍这样来培养勇气，他说：'把
胜算不大看作能够取胜。估量敌方力量相当
后再前进，考虑到能获胜再交战，这是害怕
强敌。我难道说能做到必胜吗？只不过是无
所畏惧罢了。'孟施舍像曾子，北宫黝像子夏。
这两人的勇气，不知道谁更强些，但孟施舍
掌握了关键。以前，曾子对子襄说过：'你
喜欢勇敢吗？我过去在孔子身边听到过大勇
的道理：反省义不在己，即使对方是布衣百
姓，也不去恐吓他；反省义在己，即使对方
是千万人，我也要勇往直前。'孟施舍的坚
守勇气，却比不上曾子掌握到了关键。"

（公孙丑）说："请问您的不动心和告
子的不动心，能讲给我听听吗？"

（孟子）说："告子曾说：'没有得到
社会认可的言论（舆情），不要求得心理上
的认同；没有得到心理上的认同，不要求得

气的增生。’没有得到心理上的认同，不要求得气的增生，是可以的；没有得到社会认可的言论，不要求得心理上的认同，是不可以的。心志，是主导气的；气，充斥在整个身体中。心志到哪个地方，气就留驻到哪个地方。所以说：‘控制住心志，不要滥用气。’”

（公孙丑）问："既说‘心志到哪个地方，气就留驻到哪个地方’，又说‘要控制住心志，不要滥用气’，为什么这么说呢？"

（孟子）说："心志专一就会调动气，气专一就会触动心志。比方说跌倒、奔跑，这是气在动，反过来也会扰动心志。"

（公孙丑说：）"请问，您对哪一方面比较擅长呢？"

（孟子）说："我会辨明各种言论，我善于培养我的浩然之气。"

（公孙丑说：）"请问什么叫浩然之气呢？"

（孟子）说："这很难说明白。它作为

一种气，非常浩大又十分刚强，靠正直培养它而不损害它，那就会充满于天地之间。它作为一种气，要与义和道相互配合；没有这些时，它就会疲弱。它是不断积聚正义而产生的，不是偶然一次正义的行为就得到的。如果行为有愧对之处，气就疲弱了。所以我说，告子之前不懂义，因为他把义当作心外之物。一定要好好培养义，而不能停止，心里一定不能忘记它，也不能随意助长它。不要像宋国人那样，宋国有个人担心他的禾苗长不快而去拔高它，非常疲倦地回到家中，对家人说：'今天好累啊，我帮助禾苗长高了！'他的儿子便跑到田里去看，禾苗已经枯死了。天下不助苗生长的人少啊。培养浩然之气，没有好处而放弃的人，就像不耕耘禾苗的懒汉；妄自帮助禾苗生长的人，就像拔苗助长的人一样。不但没有任何益处，而又害了它。"

（公孙丑说：）"什么叫辨明各种言论呢？"

　　（孟子）说："听到偏执的言论时，知道它片面性之所在；听到过分的言论时，知道它陷入错误之所在；听到邪恶歪曲的言论时，知道它背离正道之所在；听到逃避的言论时，知道它理屈之所在。这四种言辞，由内心生发出来的，会损害政治；而一旦显露在政治上，就要危害国家大事。若是圣人复生，一定会听信我的言论。"

　　（公孙丑说：）"宰我、子贡擅长辞令，冉牛、闵子、颜渊擅长阐述道德伦理。孔子兼有这两方面，却说：'我对于辞令，是不擅长的。'那么老师已经是圣人了吗？"

　　（孟子）说："哎呀！这是说的什么话？过去子贡问孔子说：'老师是圣人了吧？'孔子说：'圣人我做不到，我只是学习不满足，教诲别人不厌倦。'子贡说：'学而不厌是智慧，教人不倦是仁德。既有仁德又有智慧，老师已经是圣人了。'圣人，连孔子尚且不敢自称，你这是什么话？"

（公孙丑说：）"以前我私下里听说过：
子夏、子游、子张具有孔子的一部分特征，
冉牛、闵子、颜渊大体近于孔子，只是还显
得微小而不够广大。请问您属于哪一类呢？"

（孟子）说："暂且不讨论这个话题了。"

（公孙丑）问："伯夷、伊尹这俩人怎
么样呢？"

（孟子）说："处世之道不同。不是他
所期望的君主就不去服侍，不是他所期待的
百姓就不去使唤；天下稳定太平时就入朝做
官，动荡不安时就辞官隐居，这是伯夷。可
以服侍不理想的君王，可以使唤不理想的百
姓，太平盛世去做官，动荡不安也去做官，
这是伊尹。可以做官时就做官，可以辞官时
就辞官，可以长久留任就长久留任，可以马
上辞官就马上辞官，这是孔子。这些都是古
代的圣人，我还未能做到那样，至于我的愿望，
那就是学习孔子。"

（公孙丑说：）"伯夷、伊尹和孔子相比，

是一样的吗？"

（孟子）说："不。自有人类以来，没有人比得上孔子。"

（公孙丑）问："那么，他们有相同之处吗？"

（孟子）说："有啊。假设只有方圆百里的地方让他们做君主，他们都能让诸侯来朝见，坐拥天下；假设让他们做不讲道义的事情，杀一个无辜之人来得到天下，他们都不会去做的。这是他们的相同之处。"

（公孙丑）说："请问他们的不同之处呢？"

（孟子）说："宰我、子贡、有若，这三人的才智足以了解圣人，即使污下，也不至于阿谀奉承他们所喜好的人。宰我说：'凭借我对老师的观察，老师比尧、舜贤多了。'子贡说：'见到一国的礼制，就能知道该国的政治；听到一国的音乐，就能知道该国的德教。即使在百代以后，来评价百代中的君王，

没有人能违离孔子的这一观察总结。自有人
类以来，没有比孔子更伟大的了。'有若说：
'难道只是人类这样？麒麟相对于走兽，凤
凰相对于飞鸟，泰山相对于土堆，河海相对
于水沟，都是相同类别的。圣人相对于普通
人，也是同类的。都出于同类，但远远超出
了他的同类。自有人类以来，没有比孔子更
伟大的了。'"

【解读】本章篇幅较长，涉及内容较多，其中
谈有"勇""气""志""不动心"以及"养""正
气""浩然之气"等概念，厘清它们之间的
关系对于正确理解本章至关重要。一切始于
公孙丑所问"动心否"，然后由"养勇"谈
及"养气""养浩然正气"以及引申出"不
得于言，勿求于心"等一系列问题。孟子首
先通过北宫黝、孟施舍、曾子之勇分析勇之
间的差异。所谓"勇"，就是"能无惧而已
矣"；所谓"养勇"，就是把勇经过长期磨

炼形成个人的气质；这个"气"，就是指一个人的勇气。勇气之养决定着"守气""守约"的境界，进而有了"动心"与"不动心"的心理状态，"不动心"即为"不受外在的任何刺激而动摇其心"。据焦循《孟子正义》注云"养勇即养气"，也就是说"养勇""养气"都是一种培养勇气的精神活动，是儒家修身的主要内容，其最高层次便是养出"浩然正气"。有了浩然正气，自然便会产生"不动心"的心理状态。孟子对北宫黝、孟施舍、曾子之间的比较，层层递进，具有内在的逻辑关系，且价值观体现在一个"义"字当中。北宫黝养的是"不肤桡，不目逃"的匹夫之勇，孟施舍养的是"视不胜犹胜也"的"守气"之勇，曾子养的是"自反而缩，虽千万人，吾往矣"义字当先的"守约"之勇。这些养勇之法，也造就了他们"不动心"的差别。"不动心"并非指波澜不惊，而是一种通过修炼内心达到泰然处之的精神状态。进而孟子又把自己与告子的"不动心"做了比较，并在告子观点的基础上指出了他们之间的差异："不得于心，勿求于气，可；不得于言，勿求于心，不可。"为什么孟子不同意告子的"不得于言，勿求于心"呢？要想正确理解其中之"言"，还得通篇考虑此话的语境。此语是紧接北宫黝、孟施舍、曾子养勇而出，故此"言"不能单纯地当作道理或学说来看，而应该把它放在礼乐制度的大环境之中考量。曾子把"义"纳入了养勇的范畴，所以此"言"是指有道义、得到社会认可的言论。因为告子持性无善无不善论，认为人的内心"善义"是由合乎礼制的言论所引导的，不是内心本有的；而孟子是持性善论的内义观点，因此孟子不认同告子"没有得到社会认可的言论，不要求得心里的认同"的说辞。

弄通了孟子与告子"不动心"的差异，还要明白"志"与"气"之间的互动关系。我们一般讲"志"，大可理解为心志，但《孟子》

一书是把心、志分别来用的，其言心多指"道德之心"，"心"也就有了价值判断的导航性，即自觉分辨是非善恶，这当然须要"修心"才能做到。那么，"志"就是践行由心而来的道德方向，故而自古就有"志向"这一说辞。志，是一种心理活动，而"气"则属于生理活动，它们之间相互作用、相互影响的原理早为人们所知，只不过孟子研究得更透彻，故而有了"志壹则动气，气壹则动志也。今夫蹶者趋者，是气也，而反动其心"的结论。

3.3

孟子曰："以力假 [1] 仁者霸，霸必有大
国，以德行仁者王，王不待 [2] 大。汤以七十
里，文王以百里。以力服人者，非心服也，
力不赡 [3] 也；以德服人者，中心悦而诚服也，
如七十子之服孔子也。《诗》云：'自西自东，
自南自北，无思不服。'此之谓也。"

Mencius said, "He who, using force, makes a
pretence to benevolence is the leader of the princes.
A leader of the princes requires a large kingdom.
He who, using virtue, practises benevolence is the
sovereign of the kingdom. To become the sovereign
of the kingdom, a prince need not wait for a large
kingdom. Tang did it with only seventy *li*, and
king Wen with only a hundred. When one by force
subdues men, they do not submit to him in heart.
They submit, because their strength is not adequate

to resist. When one subdues men by virtue, in their hearts' core they are pleased, and sincerely submit, as was the case with the seventy disciples in their submission to Confucius. What is said in the *Book of Poetry*, 'From the west, from the east, From the south, from the north, There was not one who thought of refusing submission,' is an illustration of this."

【注释】［1］假：借。［2］待：凭靠。［3］赡：足。

【译文】孟子说："依靠武力假借仁的名义统一天下叫作'霸'，称霸一定要有强大的国力，依靠道德施行仁政而统一天下叫作'王'，称王不用凭靠强大的国力。商汤凭借七十里的土地称王，文王凭借百里的土地称王。靠武力使人服从，并不是真心服从，只是力量不足以反抗；凭借道德使人信服，百姓心悦诚服，就像孔子的弟子信服孔子一样。《诗经》

说：'从西到东，从南到北，无不心悦诚服。'
说的就是这个意思。"

【解读】本章阐述"霸"与"王"的区别。其
实质还是强调推行仁政，劝导执政者以德服
人。在孟子看来，行"霸道"，需要一个强
大的国力作为支撑；行"王道"却不必如此，
故成汤以七十里土地而成就王业，周文王以
百里土地而成就王业。实行"霸道"的本质
是以力服人，以力服人虽可能立竿见影，却
不能保证长久服从，不过是对方"力不赡也"。
正如周厉王止谤，使得"国人莫敢言，道路
以目"，最终却落得被流放的下场。以德服人，
才会长治久安，也能令人心悦诚服，像孔子
弟子服于孔子一样，矢志不渝。孟子的"以
德服人"和"王道"代表了一种至高、至善
的治国思想，但对于现实情况来讲，确实有
些不切实际，不过这种信条一直是儒家坚守
并崇尚的原则。

3.4

孟子曰："仁则荣，不仁则辱。今恶辱而居不仁，是犹恶湿而居下也。如恶之，莫如贵德而尊士，贤者在位，能者在职。国家闲暇[1]，及是时明其政刑。虽大国，必畏之矣。《诗》云：'迨[2]天之未阴雨，彻[3]彼桑土[4]，绸缪牖户[5]。今此下民，或敢侮予？'孔子曰：'为此诗者，其知道乎！能治其国家，谁敢侮之？'今国家闲暇，及是时般乐怠敖[6]，是自求祸也。祸福无不自己求之者。《诗》云：'永言配命，自求多福。'《太甲》曰：'天作孽，犹可违；自作孽，不可活。'此之谓也。"

Mencius said, "Benevolence brings glory to a prince, and the opposite of it brings disgrace. For the princes of the present day to hate disgrace and yet to live complacently doing what is not benevolent, is like hating moisture and yet living in a low situation. If a prince hates disgrace, the best course for him to pursue, is to esteem virtue and honour virtuous scholars, giving the worthiest among them places of dignity, and the able offices of trust. When throughout his kingdom there is leisure and rest from external troubles, let him, taking advantage of such a season, clearly digest the principles of his government with its legal sanctions, and then even great kingdoms will be constrained to stand in awe of him. It is said in the *Book of Poetry*, 'Before the heavens were dark with rain, I gathered the bark from the roots of the mulberry trees, And wove it closely to form the window and door of my nest; Now, I thought, ye people below, Perhaps ye will not dare to insult me.' Confucius said, 'Did not he who made this ode understand the way of governing?' If a prince is able rightly to govern his kingdom, who will dare to insult him? But now the princes take advantage of the time when throughout their kingdoms there is leisure and rest from external troubles, to abandon themselves to pleasure and indolent indifference; —they in fact seek for calamities for themselves. Calamity and happiness in all cases are men's own seeking. This is illustrated by what is said in the *Book of Poetry*, —'Be always studious to be in harmony with the ordinances of God, So you will certainly get for yourself much happiness;' and by the passage of the *Tai Jia*, 'When Heaven sends down calamities, it is still possible to escape from them; when we occasion the calamities ourselves, it is not possible any longer to live.'"

【注释】［1］闲暇：指国家安定、无内忧外患之时。［2］迨（dài）：趁着。［3］彻：剥取。［4］桑土：《韩诗》作"桑杜"，桑杜即桑树根。［5］绸缪（móu）：缠结。牖（yǒu）：窗子。户：小门。［6］般（pán）乐：大肆作乐。怠：怠惰。敖：遨游。

【译文】孟子说："施行仁政就会获得尊荣，不施行仁政就会招来耻辱。现在的人厌恶耻辱却又安于不仁，如同厌恶潮湿却又居于低洼的地方一样。假如真的厌恶耻辱，就不如崇尚仁德，尊敬读书人，让贤德的人处在官位，有才能的人有职务。趁国家无内忧外患之时，修明政治和法律制度。（这样做了，）即使是大国也会畏惧你。《诗经》说：'趁着天没下雨，剥取桑树根的皮，修补好窗子和门户。住在下面的人，谁敢欺侮我？'孔子说：'写这首诗的人，知道其中的道理！能够治理好自己的国家，谁敢欺侮呢？'如今国家没有内忧外患，在这个时候只知大肆作乐，怠惰游玩，这是自找灾祸。祸与福，无不是自己找来的。《诗经》说：'长久地与天命相配合，自己寻求更多的福禄。'《尚书·太甲》说：'上天降下的灾难，还可逃避；自己造成的罪孽，不可生也。'说的就是这个意思。"

【解读】本章体现孟子的荣辱观，又从攘除祸患的角度，论述了仁政的重要性。孟子提出，君主若不想招致耻辱，做到长治久安就必须做好两方面的事情：一是"贵德而尊士"，君王要崇尚仁德，让贤能者处于尊位；二是在国家内外无祸乱之时，勤修国政，防患于未然。若在太平时期，一味享乐倦怠，高唱太平歌词，终究有一天会自己招致祸患，逃无可逃，这也成为一种历史的定律。

3.5

孟子曰："尊贤使能，俊杰在位，则天下之士皆悦而愿立于其朝矣。市廛而不征[1]，法而不廛[2]，则天下之商皆悦而愿藏于其市矣。关讥[3]而不征，则天下之旅皆悦，而愿出于其路矣。耕者助而不税[4]，则天下之农皆悦而愿耕于其野矣。廛无夫里之布[5]，则天下之民皆悦而愿为之氓[6]矣。信能行此五者，则邻国之民仰之若父母矣。率其子弟，攻其父母，自生民以来，未有能济[7]者也。如此，则无敌于天下。无敌于天下者，天吏[8]也。然而不王者，未之有也。"

Mencius said, "If a ruler give honour to men of talents and virtue and employ the able, so that offices shall all be filled by individuals of distinction and mark; —then all the scholars of the kingdom will be pleased, and wish to stand in his court. If, in the marketplace of his capital, he levy a ground rent on the shops but do not tax the goods, or enforce the proper regulations without levying a ground-rent; — then all the traders of the kingdom will be pleased, and wish to store their goods in his marketplace. If, at his frontier-passes, there be an inspection of persons, but no taxes charged on goods or other articles, then all the travellers of the kingdom will be pleased, and wish to make their tours on his roads. If he require that the husbandmen give their mutual aid to cultivate the public field, and exact no other taxes from them; —then all the husbandmen of the kingdom will be pleased, and wish to plough in his fields. If from the occupiers of the shops in his marketplace he do not exact the fine of the individual idler, or of the hamlet's quota of cloth, then all the people of the kingdom will be pleased, and wish to come and be his people. If a ruler can truly practise these five things, then the people in the neighbouring kingdoms will look up to him as a parent. From the first birth of mankind till now, never has any one led children to attack their parent, and succeeded in his design. Thus, such a ruler will not have an enemy in all the kingdom, and he who has no enemy in the kingdom is the minister of Heaven. Never has there been a ruler in such a case who did not attain to the royal dignity."

【注释】［1］廛（chán）：储藏或堆积货物的货栈。征：征税。［2］法而不廛：商人长期积压于货栈的货物，官府依法收购，以保证商人的利益。［3］讥：查问。［4］助而不税：帮助种公田的，不再另收税。助，帮助公家种公田。［5］廛：这里指民居。夫里之布：古代的一种税收名称，即"夫布""里布"，大致相当于后世的土地税、劳役税。［6］氓：指从别处移居来的移民。［7］济：成功。［8］天吏：奉天命治民之人。

【译文】孟子说："尊重贤才，任用能人，杰出的人在其位，那么，天下的士人都很高兴，愿意到这样的朝堂来做官；市场上，提供储藏或堆积货物的货栈却不征税，官府依法征购滞销的货物不使其积压，那么，天下的商人都很高兴，愿意把货物放在这样的市场上销售；关卡上，只查问而不征税，那么，天下的旅客都很高兴，愿意在这样的道路上行走；种庄稼的，凡帮助种公田的，不再另外收取田亩税，那么，天下的农民都很高兴，愿意在这样的田野上耕种；民众居住的地方，没有额外的土地税和劳役税，那么，天下的百姓都很高兴，愿意成为这里的居民。如果能够真正做到这五个方面，那么邻国的百姓都会像敬仰父母一样敬仰他。率领子弟攻打他们的父母，这种事情自从有人类以来还没有成功过。如果这样，就能无敌于天下。无敌于天下的人叫作天吏。做到这样还没有称王，是从来没有过的。"

【解读】本章孟子提出了实施王政所采取的五个方面的措施，即人才、商业、关税、农业、移民等。孟子的仁政理想在于得民心，得到天下人民的拥护，这五个方面的措施，也分别对应了不同的人群：对待士人，要吸引贤才参与国家治理；对于商人，充分照顾到他们的利益，提供优惠，以活跃经济；对于商旅，要提供方便，只是盘查不法之人，而不是盘剥他们；对于农夫，采用井田制，只需助耕公田即可，不另加税赋；对于别国移民，通过免税吸引他们前来。这五个方面的措施，由于历史的局限性，存在着不足之处，比如对于百姓，还是主张农夫耕种井田，没把握住历史的发展趋势；但是，也存在诸多难能可贵之处，比如对商人的重视，这在后世中国传统的"重农抑商"观念中显得尤其难得。总之，孟子的这几方面的措施，特别是"尊贤使能"，对于当今社会仍具有借鉴意义。

3.6

　　孟子曰："人皆有不忍人之心。先王有不忍人之心，斯有不忍人之政矣。以不忍人之心，行不忍人之政，治天下可运之掌上。所以谓人皆有不忍人之心者，今人乍见孺子将入于井，皆有怵惕恻隐[1]之心。非所以内交[2]于孺子之父母也，非所以要誉[3]于乡党朋友也，非恶其声而然也。由是观之，无恻隐之心，非人也；无羞恶之心，非人也；无辞让之心，非人也；无是非之心，非人也。恻隐之心，仁之端也；羞恶之心，义之端也；辞让之心，礼之端也；是非之心，智之端也。人之有是四端也，犹其有四体也。有是四端而自谓不能者，自贼者也；谓其君不能者，贼其君者也。凡有四端于我[4]者，知皆扩而充之矣，若火之始然[5]，泉之始达。苟能充之，足以保四海；苟不充之，不足以事父母。"

孟
子

Mencius said, "All men have a mind which cannot bear to see the sufferings of others. The ancient kings had this commiserating mind, and they, as a matter of course, had likewise a commiserating government. When with a commiserating mind was practised a commiserating government, to rule the kingdom was as easy a matter as to make anything go round in the palm. When I say that all men have a mind which cannot bear to see the sufferings of others, my meaning may be illustrated thus: —even nowadays, if men suddenly see a child about to fall into a well, they will without exception experience a feeling of alarm and distress. They will feel so, not as a ground on which they may gain the favour of the child's parents, nor as a ground on which they may seek the praise of their neighbours and friends, nor from a dislike to the reputation of having been unmoved by such a thing. From this case we may perceive that the feeling of

226

胸怀天下　李岩　绘

commiseration is essential to man, that the feeling of shame and dislike is essential to man, that the feeling of modesty and complaisance is essential to man, and that the feeling of approving and disapproving is essential to man. The feeling of commiseration is the principle of benevolence. The feeling of shame and dislike is the principle of righteousness. The feeling of modesty and complaisance is the principle of propriety. The feeling of approving and disapproving is the principle of knowledge. Men have these four principles just as they have their four limbs. When men, having these four principles, yet say of themselves that they cannot develop them, they play the thief with themselves, and he who says of his prince that he cannot develop them plays the thief with his prince. Since all men have these four principles in themselves, let them know to give them all their development and completion, and the issue will be like that of fire which has begun to burn, or that of a spring which has begun to find vent. Let them have their complete development, and they will suffice to love and protect all within the four seas. Let them be denied that development, and they will not suffice for a man to serve his parents with."

【注释】［1］怵惕（chù tì）：恐惧。恻隐：同情，怜悯。［2］内（nà）交：即结交。内：同"纳"。［3］要誉：博取名誉。要：同"邀"，求。［4］我：同"己"。［5］然：同"燃"。

【译文】孟子说："每个人都有怜悯体恤他人之心。先王有怜悯体恤他人之心，所以有怜悯体恤百姓的政治。用怜悯体恤他人的心情，施行怜悯体恤百姓的政治，治理天下就可以像运转手心的东西一样容易了。之所以说每个人都有怜悯体恤他人之心，（是因为）现在有人忽见一个小孩快要掉进井里，都会产生惊恐怜悯的心情。这并不是想要和孩子的

父母结交，不是为了在乡邻朋友中博取名誉，
也不是因为厌恶这孩子的哭叫声才这样的。
由此看来，没有同情心，就不是人；没有羞
耻心，就不是人；没有谦让心，就不是人；
没有是非心，就不是人。同情心，是仁的发端；
羞耻心，是义的发端；谦让心，是礼的发端；
是非心，是智的发端。人有这四种发端，就
像有四肢一样。有了这四种发端却自认为不
行的人，是自己残害自己的人；认为他的君
主不行的人，是戕害君主的人。凡是自己有
这四种发端的人，就该知道将它扩大充实起
来，就像火刚刚开始燃烧，泉水刚刚开始流
淌一样。如果能够将它扩充，便足以安定天下；
如果不能扩充，连赡养父母都办不到。"

【解读】本章孟子鲜明地提出了"四心"说来
论述人的本性。孟子首先肯定"人皆有不忍
人之心"，然后通过救落井孩子的例子，让
我们明白了每个人都具有"恻隐之心"的道理，

所以执政者施行仁政也天经地义。并推而广之指出，人具有恻隐之心、羞恶之心、辞让之心、是非之心，这是人的本性；而这四心又是仁、义、礼、智的四种发端。每个人都具有将这四端"扩而充之"的可能性，只不过有些人不去做罢了。如果能够扩充自己先天具有的"四端"，便可以保全四海；如果不加以扩充，甚至不足以侍奉父母。只有将"四心"存于心，以"四德"律于己，才能够不断地完善自己的道德修养，提高自己的道德境界，以至成为圣人。

"四心"说在孟子"性善论"中处于基础性地位，而"性善论"正是孟子思想体系中重要的组成部分，所以理解"四心"说对于理解孟子的思想意义重大。

3.7

孟子曰："矢人岂不仁于函人哉[1]？矢人唯恐不伤人，函人唯恐伤人。巫匠[2]亦然。故术[3]不可不慎也。孔子曰：'里仁为美。择不处仁，焉得智？'夫仁，天之尊爵也，人之安宅也。莫之御[4]而不仁，是不智也。不仁、不智、无礼、无义，人役也。人役而耻为役，由弓人而耻为弓，矢人而耻为矢也。如耻之，莫如为仁。仁者如射，射者正己而后发。发而不中，不怨胜己者，反求诸己而已矣。"

Mencius said, "Is the arrow-maker less benevolent than the maker of armour of defence? And yet, the arrow-maker's only fear is lest men should not be hurt, and the armour-maker's only fear is lest men should be hurt. So it is with the priest and the coffin-maker. The choice of a profession, therefore, is a thing in which great caution is required. Confucius said, 'It is virtuous manners which constitute the excellence of a neighbourhood. If a man, in selecting a residence, do not fix on one where such prevail, how can he be wise?' Now, benevolence is the most honourable dignity conferred by Heaven, and the quiet home in which man should dwell. Since no one can hinder us from being so, if yet we are not benevolent; — this is being not wise. From the want of benevolence and the want of wisdom will ensue the entire absence of propriety and righteousness; — he who is in such a case must be the servant of other men. To be the servant of men and yet ashamed of such servitude, is like a bow-maker's being ashamed to make bows, or an arrow-maker's being ashamed to make arrows. If he be ashamed of his case, his best course is to practise benevolence. The man who would be benevolent is like the archer. The archer adjusts himself and then shoots. If he misses, he does not murmur against those who surpass himself. He simply turns round and seeks the cause of his failure in himself."

【注释】［1］矢人：造箭的工匠。函人：制造铠甲的工匠。［2］巫匠：巫医和匠人。巫医为人祈祝治病，利人之生；匠人制作棺椁，利人之死。［3］术：这里指选择谋生之术，也就是选择职业。［4］御：阻挡。

【译文】孟子说："造箭的人难道比造铠甲的人不仁吗？造箭的人唯恐自己造的箭不能伤人，造铠甲的人却唯恐人被射伤。巫医和匠人之间也是这样，所以一个人谋生的职业不能不慎重选择啊。孔子说：'居住在有仁厚风气的地方为好。选择住处时不择仁厚之乡，怎么能说是明智呢？'仁，是上天赐予人们的尊贵的爵位，是人最安定的住宅。没有什么阻挡却不选择仁，是不明智的。不仁不智、无礼无义的人，只配当别人的仆役。被人役使而又觉得耻于被人役使，就像造弓的人以造弓为耻，造箭的人以造箭为耻一样。如果真正引以为耻，那就不如好好实行仁。实行仁的道理就像射箭一样，射手先端正自己的姿势然后才放箭。如果没有射中，不怨恨赢了自己的人，而是反过来在自己身上找原因罢了。"

【解读】本章孟子以"矢人""函人""巫""匠"四种谋生职业谈起，得出"术不可不慎也"的结论。然后，将职业选择推及人生道路选择，从而告诫人们当选择仁义之道。在孟子心中，"仁"具有至高无上的地位，是"天之尊爵也，人之安宅也"。如果选择了与仁义之道相反的一面，就会为人役使，甚至于会感到羞耻。如果真感到羞耻就应该砥砺行仁，不要埋怨外人，应多从自身找原因。那种自身感到羞耻却埋怨外人的行为，是怨天尤人。当然，孟子并不是要否定社会分工，主要是强调每个职业都应该行仁。行不行仁义之道关键在于自己的选择，行仁先正己，这大概也就是孟子说"反求诸己"的缘故吧。

3.8

孟子曰："子路，人告之以有过，则喜。禹闻善言则拜。大舜有 [1] 大焉，善与人同 [2]，舍己从人，乐取于人以为善。自耕、稼、陶、渔以至为帝，无非取于人者。取诸人以为善，是与人为善者也 [3]。故君子莫大乎与人为善。"

Mencius said, "When any one told Zilu that he had a fault, he rejoiced. When Yu heard good words, he bowed to the speaker. The great Shun had a still greater delight in what was good. He regarded virtue as the common property of himself and others, giving up his own way to follow that of others, and delighting to learn from others to practise what was good. From the time when he ploughed and sowed, exercised the potter's art, and was a fisherman, to the time when he became emperor, he was continually learning from others. To take example from others to

practise virtue is to help them in the same practice.
Therefore, there is no attribute of the superior man
greater than his helping men to practise virtue."

【注释】［1］有：同"又"。［2］善与人同：
善与人通，在做善事上不分人我。［3］与人
为善：同别人一起行善。今多指善意帮助别人。

【译文】孟子说："子路，听到别人指出自己
的过错，他就高兴。大禹听到有教益的话，
就向人家拜谢。舜帝又有伟大之处，对于行善，
没有别人与自己的差别，舍弃自己的不足，
学习别人的优点，乐于吸取别人的长处来行
善。从他种地、做瓦器、捕鱼一直到做帝王，
没有哪个时候他不向别人学习。吸取别人的
优点来行善，就如同与别人一起来行善。因此，
君子最重要的就是与别人一起来行善。"

【解读】本章主旨在于崇尚"与人为善"之仁的

最高境界。孟子列举了子路、禹、大舜的例子，谈论了三人生活中不同的表现，实际是指出了三种不同的人生境界：子路闻过则喜，能够不断改正自己的错误，这可以看出子路谦虚的胸怀；禹闻善则拜，听到有教益的话，就向人家拜谢，则可以看出禹追求提高的积极态度；而大舜伟大之处在于"与人为善"，能够与别人一起做善事。子路、禹都是为己，而大舜不仅为己还为他人，帮助别人一起提高，这就是儒家追求的"仁"的境界：己欲立而立人，己欲达而达人。所以，孟子说君子最重要的就是与别人一起来行善。

3.9

孟子曰："伯夷，非其君不事[1]，非其友不友[2]。不立于恶人之朝，不与恶人言。立于恶人之朝，与恶人言，如以朝衣朝冠坐于涂炭[3]。推恶恶之心，思与乡人立，其冠不正，望望然[4]去之，若将浼[5]焉。是故诸侯虽有善其辞命而至者，不受也。不受也者，是亦不屑就已。柳下惠，不羞污君，不卑小官；进[6]不隐贤，必以其道；遗佚[7]而不怨，厄[8]穷而不悯。故曰：'尔为尔，我为我，虽袒裼裸裎于我侧[9]，尔焉能浼我哉？'故由由然[10]与之偕而不自失焉，援而止之而止。援而止之而止者，是亦不屑去已。"

孟子曰："伯夷隘，柳下惠不恭。隘与不恭，君子不由[11]也。"

Mencius said, "Boyi would not serve a prince whom he did not approve, nor associate with a

friend whom he did not esteem. He would not stand
in a bad prince's court, nor speak with a bad man.
To stand in a bad prince's court, or to speak with a
bad man, would have been to him the same as to sit
with his court robes and court cap amid mire and
ashes. Pursuing the examination of his dislike to
what was evil, we find that he thought it necessary,
if he happened to be standing with a villager whose
cap was not rightly adjusted, to leave him with a
high air, as if he were going to be defiled. Therefore,
although some of the princes made application to
him with very proper messages, he would not receive
their gifts. He would not receive their gifts, counting
it inconsistent with his purity to go to them. Hui of
Liu-xia was not ashamed to serve an impure prince,
nor did he think it low to be an inferior officer.
When advanced to employment, he did not conceal
his virtue, but made it a point to carry out his
principles. When neglected and left without office,

he did not murmur. When straitened by poverty, he did not grieve. Accordingly, he had a saying, 'You are you, and I am I. Although you stand by my side with breast and aims bare, or with your body naked, how can you defile me?' Therefore, self-possessed, he companied with men indifferently, at the same time not losing himself. When he wished to leave, if pressed to remain in office, he would remain. He would remain in office, when pressed to do so, not counting it required by his purity to go away."

Mencius said, "Boyi was narrow-minded, and Hui of Liuxia was wanting in self-respect. The superior man will not manifest either narrow-mindedness，or the want of self-respect."

【注释】［1］事：同"侍"，侍奉。［2］友：结交。［3］涂炭：污泥和炭灰，比喻污浊的地方。［4］望望然：失望、扫兴的样子。［5］浼（měi）：污染。［6］进：入朝做官。［7］遗佚：遗弃而不用。[8]厄：困窘。[9]袒裼（xī）：脱去上衣，露出肢体。裸裎（chéng）：赤身裸体，谓粗野无礼。[10]由由然：高兴的样子。[11]由：遵从，效仿。

【译文】孟子说："伯夷这个人，不是他理想的君主就不去侍奉，不是他理想的朋友就不去结交。不在恶人的朝廷里做官，不与恶人交谈。在恶人的朝廷里做官，与恶人交谈，就如同穿戴着上朝的衣帽坐在污浊的地方一样。推想这种厌恶恶人的心理，想象他与乡下人站在一起，如果那人帽子不正，就扫兴地离开，就像会被那人污染一样。因此诸侯虽然用好言好语来请他做官，他却不接受。之所以不接受，是因为他不屑于接近他们。柳下惠，不以侍奉不贤明的君主为羞耻，不以官小为卑下；入朝做官不隐藏自己的才干，一定按照自己的原则；即使被遗弃不用也不埋怨，困穷也不忧伤。因此他说：'你是你，我是我，

即使你赤身裸体站在我旁边，又怎能污染我
呢？'所以他能怡然自得地与各类人处在一
起而不失去自己的原则，拉他留下他就留下。
拉他留下他就留下，也是不屑离开罢了。"

　　孟子又说："伯夷气量狭小，柳下惠有
失庄重。气量小与不庄重，君子是不会遵从
的。"

【解读】本章主要评价伯夷、柳下惠的为人处
世，并指出他们二人都有缺点，是不值得君
子效仿的。孟子认为伯夷为人原则性太强，
不符合自己的理想要求，无论什么人都不接
受，无论什么事都不将就，所以孟子评价他
有些狭隘；而柳下惠虽然也有自己的原则，
却太过随意，和什么人都可相处，受重用可
以，身处困境亦可，无可无不可，颇有和光
同尘的意味，孟子又认为他有失庄重了。在
孟子看来，伯夷、伊尹、柳下惠与孔子都是"圣
人"，只不过只有孔子懂得权变，与时偕行，

是最高级别的圣人。伯夷清高，气量狭小；柳下惠随和，有失庄重。孟子主张，君子行事要避免偏颇，把握好合适的度，坚持中庸之道。这种行事原则，至今仍有借鉴意义和实践价值。

公孙丑下

Gong Sun Chou 2

4.1

孟子曰："天时不如地利，地利不如人和 [1]。三里之城，七里之郭 [2]，环而攻之而不胜。夫环而攻之，必有得天时者矣；然而不胜者，是天时不如地利也。城非不高也，池 [3] 非不深也，兵革 [4] 非不坚利也，米粟非不多也，委 [5] 而去之，是地利不如人和也。故曰：域民 [6] 不以封疆之界，固国不以山溪 [7] 之险，威天下不以兵革之利。得道者多助，失道者寡助。寡助之至，亲戚畔 [8] 之；多助之至，天下顺之。以天下之所顺，攻亲戚之所畔，故君子有 [9] 不战，战必胜矣。"

Mencius said, "Opportunities of time vouchsafed by Heaven are not equal to advantages of situation afforded by the Earth, and advantages of situation afforded by the Earth are not equal to the union arising from the accord of Men. There is a city, with an inner wall of three *li* in circumference, and an outer wall of seven. The enemy surround and attack it, but they are not able to take it. Now, to surround and attack it, there must have been vouchsafed to them by Heaven the opportunity of time, and in such case their not taking it is because opportunities of time vouchsafed by Heaven are not equal to advantages of situation afforded by the Earth. There is a city, whose walls are distinguished for their height, and whose moats are distinguished for their depth, where the arms of its defenders, offensive and defensive, are distinguished for their strength and sharpness, and the stores of rice and other grain are very large. Yet it is obliged to be given up and abandoned. This is because advantages of situation afforded by the Earth are not equal to the union arising from the accord of Men. In accordance with these principles it is said, 'A people is bounded in, not by the limits of dykes and borders; a state is secured, not by the strengths of mountains and rivers; the kingdom is overawed, not by the sharpness and strength of arms.' He who finds the proper course has many to assist him. He who loses the proper course has few to assist him. When this, —the being assisted by few, —reaches its extreme point, his own relations revolt from the prince. When the being assisted by many reaches its highest point, the whole kingdom becomes obedient to the prince. When one to whom the whole kingdom is prepared to be obedient, attacks those from whom their own relations revolt, what must be the result? Therefore, the true ruler will prefer not to fight; but if he do fight, he must overcome."

【注释】 [1] 天时、地利、人和：孟子在这里所说的"天时"是指作战的时机，包括时令、气候，乃至政治形势等非人力所能及的条件；"地利"是指有利于作战的地理条件；"人和"

则指人心所向、内部团结等。[2]郭：外城墙，
在内城墙外加筑的城墙。[3]池：护城河。
[4]兵革：泛指武器装备。[5]委：放弃。
[6]域民：限制人民。域：界限。[7]山溪：
山岭沟壑。[8]畔：同"叛"，背叛。[9]
有：或，要么。

【译文】 孟子说："有利的天气和时机不如有
利的地势，有利的地势不如作战中人心所向、
内部团结。一个方圆三里的内城、七里的外
城，四面围攻却不能够攻破。既然四面围攻它，
一定有得天时的机会；然而不能取胜，这是
天时不如地利啊。城墙并非不高，护城河并
非不深，武器装备并非不精良，粮食供给并
非不充足，但还是弃城而逃了，这是地利不
如人和啊。所以说：限制百姓外逃，不能靠
划定疆域的界限；巩固国防，不能靠山岭沟
壑的险要；威慑天下，不能靠武器的锋利。
占据道义的人，能得到众多人的帮助；失去

天时不如地利，地利不如人和　韦辛夷　绘

道义的人，得到的帮助就少。帮助的人少到极点时，连亲戚也会叛离；帮助的人多到极点时，全天下的人都会顺从。以全天下人都顺从的力量去攻打连亲戚都会叛离的人，君子要么不战斗，进行战斗就一定会取得胜利。"

【解读】本章孟子从军事方面分析得出一个光耀千古的观点：天时不如地利，地利不如人和。任何的天时、地利都比不上人和，这是由人具有主观能动性所决定的。人和就是顺民意，得民心，民众团结一致。自古及今，只要统治者能坚守道义，施仁政于民，定会是民心所向，得道多助，进而赢得天下。周文王仁爱天下，民心攒聚；武王伐纣，八百诸侯"赢粮而景从"。风雨兼程二十八载，中国共产党从弱小走向强大，"星星之火"成了燎原之势，其中一场淮海战役，就是老百姓用小推车推出来的胜利，是人民战争胜利的缩影，是民心的胜利。而"和"的理念也体现了中国人独有的"尚和合"的文化人格。当今时代，人类需要探索合理的国际新秩序，中国的这种"尚和合"的精神有着无与伦比的魅力，无论是郑和七次下西洋的壮举，还是中华人民共和国成立伊始深得世界人民之心的和平共处五项原则，还是当今"建设人类命运共同体"的庄严宣告，都是热爱和平的中国人民对世界的贡献！

张 博 制

4.2

孟子将朝王[1]，王使人来曰："寡人如[2]就见者也，有寒疾，不可以风。朝将视朝[3]，不识[4]可使寡人得见乎？"

对曰："不幸而有疾，不能造[5]朝。"

明日出吊于东郭氏[6]。公孙丑曰："昔者辞以病，今日吊，或者不可乎？"

曰："昔者疾，今日愈，如之何不吊？"

王使人问疾，医来。

孟仲子[7]对曰："昔者有王命，有采薪之忧[8]，不能造朝。今病小愈，趋造于朝，我不识能至否乎？"

使数人要[9]于路，曰："请必无归，而造于朝！"

不得已而之景丑氏[10]宿焉。

景子曰："内则父子，外则君臣，人之大伦也。父子主恩，君臣主敬。丑见王之敬子也，未见所以敬王也。"

曰："恶！是何言也！齐人无以仁义与王言者，岂以仁义为不美也？其心曰'是何足与言仁义也'云尔，则不敬莫大乎是。我非尧舜之道，不敢以陈于王前，故齐人莫如我敬王也。"

景子曰："否，非此之谓也。《礼》曰：'父召，无诺[11]；君命召，不俟驾[12]。'固将朝也，闻王命而遂不果，宜[13]与夫礼若不相似然。"

曰："岂谓是与？曾子曰：'晋、楚之富，不可及也。彼以其富，我以吾仁；彼以其爵，我以吾义。吾何慊[14]乎哉？'夫岂不义而曾子言之？是或一道也。天下有达尊三：爵一，齿一，德一。朝廷莫如爵，乡党莫如齿，辅世长民莫如德。恶得有其一以慢其二哉？故将大有为之君，必有所不召之臣。欲有谋焉，则就之。其尊德乐道不如是，不足与有为也。故汤之于伊尹，学焉而后臣之，故不劳而王；桓公之于管仲，学焉而后臣之，故不劳而霸。今天下地丑[15]德齐，莫能相尚。无他，好臣

其所教 [16]，而不好臣其所受教。汤之于伊尹，桓公之于管仲，则不敢召。管仲且犹不可召，而况不为管仲者乎？"

As Mencius was about to go to court to see the king, the king sent a person to him with this message:—"I was wishing to come and see you. But I have got a cold, and may not expose myself to the wind. In the morning I will hold my court. I do not know whether you will give me the opportunity of seeing you then."

Mencius replied, "Unfortunately, I am unwell, and not able to go to the court."

Next day, he went out to pay a visit of condolence to some one of the Dongguo family, when Gongsun Chou said to him, "Yesterday, you declined going to the court on the ground of being unwell, and today you are going to pay a visit of condolence. May this not be regarded as improper?"

"Yesterday," said Mencius, "I was unwell;

today, I am better: —why should I not pay this visit?"

In the mean time, the king sent a messenger to inquire about his sickness, and also a physician.

Meng Zhong replied to them, "Yesterday, when the king's order came, he was feeling a little unwell, and could not go to the court. Today he was a little better, and hastened to go to court. I do not know whether he can have reached it by this time or not."

Having said this, he sent several men to look for Mencius on the way, and say to him, "I beg that, before you return home, you will go to the court."

On this, Mencius felt himself compelled to go to Jing Chou's, and there stop the night.

Mr. Jing said to him, "In the family, there is the relation of father and son; abroad, there is the relation of prince and minister. These are the two great relations among men. Between father and son the ruling principle is kindness. Between prince and minister the ruling principle is respect. I have seen the respect of the king to you, Sir, but I have not seen in what way you show respect to him."

Mencius replied, "Oh! what words are these? Among the people of Qi there is no one who speaks to the king about benevolence and righteousness. Are they thus silent because they do not think that benevolence and righteousness are admirable? No, but in their hearts they say, 'This man is not fit to be spoken with about benevolence and righteousness.' Thus they manifest a disrespect than which there can be none greater. I do not dare to set forth before the king any but the ways of Yao and Shun. There is therefore no man of Qi who respects the king so much as I do."

Mr. Jing said, "Not so. That was not what I meant. In the *Book of Rites* it is said, 'When a father calls, the answer must be without a moment's hesitation. When the prince's order calls, the carriage must not be waited for.' You were certainly going to the court, but when you heard the king's order, then you did not carry your purpose out. This does seem as if it were not in accordance with that rule of propriety."

Mencius answered him, "How can you give that meaning to my conduct? The philosopher Zeng said, 'The wealth of Jin and Chu cannot be equalled. Let their rulers have their wealth: — I have my benevolence. Let them have their nobility: —I have my righteousness. Wherein should I be dissatisfied as inferior to them?' Now shall we say that these sentiments are not right? Seeing that the philosopher Zeng spoke them, there is in them, I apprehend a real principle. In the kingdom there are three things universally acknowledged to be honourable. Nobility is one of them; age is one of them; virtue is one of them. In courts, nobility holds the first place of the three; in villages, age holds the first place;

and for helping one's generation and presiding over the people, the other two are not equal to virtue. How can the possession of only one of these be presumed on to despise one who possesses the other two? Therefore a prince who is to accomplish great deeds will certainly have ministers whom he does not call to go to him. When he wishes to consult with them, he goes to them. The prince who does not honour the virtuous, and delight in their ways of doing, to this extent, is not worth having to do with. Accordingly, there was the behaviour of Tang to Yi-yin: —he first learned of him, and then employed him as his minister; and so without difficulty he became sovereign. There was the behaviour of the duke Huan to Guan Zhong: —he first learned of him, and then employed him as his minister; and so without difficulty he became chief of all the princes. Now throughout the kingdom, the territories of the princes are of equal extent, and in their achievements they are on a level. Not one of them is able to exceed the others. This is from no other reason, but that they love to make ministers of those whom they teach, and do not love to make ministers of those by whom they might be taught. So did Tang behave to Yiyin, and the duke Huan to Guan Zhong, that they would not venture to call them to go to them. If Guan Zhong might not be called to him by his prince, how much less may he be called, who would not play the part of Guan Zhong!"

【注释】[1]王：指齐王。[2]如：宜，应当。[3]朝将视朝：第一个"朝"读 zhāo，即"清晨"。第二个"朝"读 cháo，即"朝廷"。视朝：即在朝廷处理政务。[4]不识：不知。[5]造：到。[6]东郭氏：齐国大夫。[7]孟仲子：孟子的堂兄弟，跟随孟子学习。[8]采薪之忧：本意是说生病不能去打柴，引申为自称生病。[9]要（yāo）：半路拦截。[10]景丑氏：

齐国大夫。［11］父召，无诺：“唯”和“诺”都是表示应答，急时用“唯”，缓时用“诺”。父召无诺的意思是说，听到父亲召唤，不能慢吞吞答应。［12］不俟驾：不等到车马备好，就急匆匆步行先走。［13］宜：大概，恐怕。［14］慊（qiàn）：憾，不满足。［15］丑：类似，等同。［16］所教：听从于己者。

【译文】孟子正准备去朝见齐王，此时齐王派人来转达说：“我本应该来看您，但是受了风寒，不可以见风。明早我将上朝处理政务，不知您能否来朝廷上，让我见到您？”

（孟子回答）说：“不幸的是，我也得了病，不能到朝。”

第二天，孟子要到东郭大夫家里去吊丧。公孙丑说：“昨天您托病谢绝了齐王的召见，今天却又去东郭大夫家里吊丧，这或许不太合适吧？”

（孟子）说：“昨天生病，今天好了，

为什么不可以去吊丧？"

齐王派人来问候孟子的病情，并且带来
了医生。

孟仲子应付说："昨天大王命令来时，
他正生着病，不能到朝。今天病刚好了一点，
已经上朝去了，但我不知道到了没有。"

孟仲子立即派人到路上去拦截孟子，转
告孟子说："请一定不要回家，赶快上朝廷
去！"

孟子不得已，躲到景丑的家里去歇宿。

景丑说："在家有父子，在外有君臣，
这是最重要的伦理关系。父子之间以慈恩为
主，君臣之间以恭敬为主。我只看见齐王尊
敬您，却没看见您尊敬齐王。"

（孟子）说："哎！这是什么话！在齐
国人中没有一个与齐王谈论仁义的，难道是
他们觉得仁义不好吗？他们心里想的是'这
样的国君哪里值得和他谈论仁义'，如此而已，
这才是他们对齐王最大的不恭敬。我不是尧

舜之道就不敢在齐王面前陈述，所以齐国人没有谁比我更尊敬齐王了。"

景丑说："不，我不是说的这个方面。《礼》上说：'父亲召唤，不能慢吞吞地应"诺"；君王召唤，不等车马备好就急匆匆跑步前行。'可您呢，本来就准备朝见齐王，听到齐王的召见反而不去了，这似乎和礼法不大相符吧。"

（孟子）说："难道你说的是这个？曾子说过：'晋国和楚国的财富，没有哪个国家赶得上。不过，他凭借他的财富，我凭借我的仁；他凭借他的爵位，我凭借我的道义。我有什么遗憾的呢？'不义的话，曾子会说吗？这话也许有一番道理吧。天下有三样最尊贵的东西：一是爵位，一是年龄，一是德行。在朝廷上，莫如爵位；在乡里，莫如年龄；至于辅助君王长养百姓，莫如德行。怎么能够只占了其中一个就怠慢其他两个呢？所以，大有作为的君主一定有他不能随意召唤的大臣，如果他有什么事情需要出谋划策，就亲自去拜访他们。这就叫尊重德行喜爱仁道，不这样就不能够大有作为。因此，商汤对于伊尹，先向他学习，而后以他为臣，所以不劳费大力气就统一了天下；桓公对于管仲，也是先向他学习，而后以他为臣，所以不劳费大力气就称霸于诸侯。现在天下各国的土地都差不多，君主的德行也相当，相互间谁也超不过谁，没有别的原因，就是因为君王们只喜欢用听他们话的人为臣，而不喜欢用能够教导他们的人为臣。商汤对于伊尹，桓公对于管仲，就不敢随意召唤。管仲尚且不可以被随意召唤，更何况是连管仲都不屑为伍的人呢？"

【解读】"将大有为之君，必有所不召之臣。"铿锵有力的一句话穿越古今，吼出了两千多年里仁人志士的铮铮风骨。齐王病了，取消了和孟子的见面，从而引出了孟子谎称生病，

是孟子生气了吗？齐王第二天派人问候孟子
并派来了医生，可见齐王的礼数到了，而孟
子竟然又躲了起来，这是孟子的任性吗？非
也！孟子欲做不召之臣，欲寻有为之君。人
有财富我有仁义，人有爵位我有仁义，不管
面前是金山还是王侯，"富贵于我如浮云"，
满足于仁义就行了，这就是不被景丑等人理
解的孟子。

　　齐宣王面对一般的贤者，礼数已经很好
了，但想要做大有作为的君主，必定有他不
能随意召见的臣子，需要亲自前去请教。齐
宣王最终也没有理解孟子的苦心，不能称孟
子的意。孟子胸怀大略，期望齐王成为大有
作为的君主，最起码要比得上齐桓公，因为
自己要做比管仲更强的人。历史上的商汤之
于伊尹，桓公于管仲，他们无不礼贤下士，
主动请教，这是孟子所向往的，但他又不屑
与管仲为伍，故而说出了"管仲且犹不可召，
而况不为管仲者乎"。前有周文王屈尊求贤

姜子牙于渭水之滨，方得存周八百余载；后有三国刘玄德三顾茅庐，放下身段做学生，终成三足鼎立而彪炳史册。"大有为之君"的用人之道一直贯穿于我国的历史之中，并产生积极的影响。

4.3

陈臻[1]问曰:"前日于齐,王馈兼金[2]一百而不受;于宋,馈七十镒而受;于薛,馈五十镒而受。前日之不受是,则今日之受非也;今日之受是,则前日之不受非也。夫子必居一于此矣。"

孟子曰:"皆是也。当在宋也,予将有远行。行者必以赆[3],辞曰:'馈赆。'予何为不受?当在薛也,予有戒心[4]。辞曰:'闻戒。'故为兵馈之,予何为不受?若于齐,则未有处[5]也。无处而馈之,是货之也。焉有君子而可以货[6]取乎?"

Chen Zhen asked Mencius, saying, "Formerly, when you were in Qi, the king sent you a present of 2,400 taels of fine silver, and you refused to accept it. When you were in Song, 1,680 taels were sent to you, which you accepted; and when you were in Xue, 1,200 taels were sent, which you likewise accepted. If your declining to accept the gift in the first case was right, your accepting it in the latter cases was wrong. If your accepting it in the latter cases was right, your declining to do so in the first case was wrong. You must accept, Master, one of these alternatives."

Mencius said, "I did right in all the cases. When I was in Song, I was about to take a long journey. Travellers must be provided with what is necessary for their expenses. The prince's message was, 'A present against travelling-expenses.' Why should I have declined the gift? When I was in Xue, I was apprehensive for my safety, and taking measures for my protection. The message was, 'I have heard that you are taking measures to protect yourself, and send this to help you in procuring arms.' Why should I have declined the gift? But when I was in Qi, I had no occasion for money. To send a man a gift when he has no occasion for it, is to bribe him. How is it possible that a superior man should be taken with a bribe?"

【注释】［1］陈臻：孟子的学生。［2］兼金：成色上好的金子，因其价格双倍于普通金，所以称为"兼金"。［3］赆（jìn）：给远行人的盘缠或礼物。［4］戒心：戒备之心。［5］处：享有，据有。［6］货：收买，贿赂。

【译文】陈臻问孟子说："以前在齐国，齐王送您一百镒上等金您不接受；在宋国，宋国国君给您七十镒却接受了；在薛地，薛君送给您五十镒您也接受了。如果以前不接受是正确的，那么今天接受就是错误的；如果今天接受是正确的，那么以前不接受就是错误的。这两种情况中您必定有一种吧。"

孟子说："都是对的。在宋国的时候，我将要远行，对远行的人一定要送他一些盘缠，所以宋君辞别时说：'送上一些路费吧。'我为何不接受？在薛地的时候，路上有危险，我有戒备之心，薛君辞别时说：'听说您需要戒备，所以送一些买兵器的钱。'我为何不接受？至于在齐国，则没有理由享有了。没有理由享有的馈赠，这等于是收买啊。哪里有君子可以用财货收买的呢？"

【解读】孟子的一生，风骨嶙峋，视富贵如浮云，"万钟于我何加焉！"本章记载了孟子面对三次送礼的不同表现，让陈臻产生了疑惑：齐王的一百金不收，宋国的七十金、薛国的五十金反倒痛快地收下了，为什么？其实，陈臻的推理是一种形式逻辑的思维，即非此即彼的论断，缺少的是辩证逻辑思维的变通，取与不取，均有道理。齐王送的黄金，孟子觉得"师出无名"，"名不正则言不顺"，没有理由接受。俗话说"拿人家的手短"，可能会受制于人，以自由和人格为代价的钱财不取也罢。宋国给的是路费，薛国给的是关心，成人之美的帮助却之不恭，这应该是孟子的通权达变吧。

4.4

孟子之平陆[1]。谓其大夫[2]曰："子之持戟之士，一日而三失伍[3]，则去之否乎？"

曰："不待三。"

"然则子之失伍也亦多矣。凶年饥岁，子之民，老羸[4]转于沟壑，壮者散而之四方者，几千人矣。"

曰："此非距心之所得为也。"

曰："今有受人之牛羊而为之牧之者，则必为之求牧与刍矣。求牧与刍而不得，则反诸其人乎？抑亦立而视其死与？"

曰："此则距心之罪也。"

他日，见于王曰："王之为都者，臣知五人焉。知其罪者，惟孔距心。为王诵之。"

王曰："此则寡人之罪也。"

Mencius having gone to Pinglu, addressed the governor of it, saying, "If one of your spearmen should lose his place in the ranks three times in one day, would you, Sir, put him to death or not?"

"I would not wait for three times to do so," was the reply.

Mencius said, "Well then, you, Sir, have likewise lost your place in the ranks many times. In bad calamitous years, and years of famine, the old and feeble of your people, who have been found lying in the ditches and water-channels, and the able-bodied, who have been scattered about to the four quarters, have amounted to several thousand."

The governor replied, "That is a state of things in which it does not belong to me Juxin to act."

"Here," said Mencius, "is a man who receives charge of the cattle and sheep of another, and undertakes to feed them for him;— of course he must search for pasture-ground and grass for them. If, after searching for those, he cannot find them, will he return his charge to the owner? Or will he stand by and see them die?"

"Herein," said the officer, "I am guilty."

Another day, Mencius had an audience of the king, and said to him, "Of the governors of Your Majesty's cities I am acquainted with five, but the only one of them who knows his faults is Kong Ju-xin."

He then repeated the conversation to the king, who said, "In this matter, I am the guilty one."

【注释】[1]平陆：齐国边境城邑名，故址在今山东汶上县北。[2]大夫：指当地长官，即下文所言孔距心。[3]失伍：掉队，擅离职守。[4]羸（léi）：瘦弱。

【译文】孟子来到了平陆。对那里的长官（孔距心）说："如果您的战士一天三次擅离职守，开除他吗？"

（孔距心）说："不必等到三次。"

（孟子说：）"那么您失职的地方也够多的了。荒年饥岁，您的百姓中年老体弱的因饥饿辗转而死在山野沟壑里，身强体壮的便逃散到四方，应该有近千人吧。"

（孔距心）说："这种事情不是我能够解决的。"

（孟子）说："假如现在有个人接受了别人的牛羊而替他放牧，那么必定要为牛羊寻找牧场和草料。如果找不到牧场和草料，那么是把牛羊还给那个人呢，还是就站在那儿眼看着牛羊饿死呢？"

（孔距心）说："这是我的罪过。"

他日，孟子见到齐王，说："大王的地方长官我认识五人，能认识自己罪过的，只有孔距心。于是为齐王讲述了与孔距心对话的事。"

齐王说："这是我的罪过啊。"

【解读】本章通过孟子与地方官员的对话，巧妙地表达了一个鲜明的政治理念，就是为政者无论官位高低，都应恪尽职守，关心民众疾苦，不能对百姓的死活不负责任，甚至无动于衷。

孟子用管理牛羊要负责它们的死活作类比，让平陆的长官孔距心和齐王都心服口服地承认了自己的错误，但从以后的齐国现实来看，并没有落实到行动中。在那个弱肉强食的战乱时代，战争阴云密布，"霸道"思想无孔不入，施行仁政，似乎是空中楼阁。

4.5

孟子谓蚳蛙[1]曰："子之辞灵丘而请士师[2]，似也，为其可以言也。今既数月矣，未可以言与？"

蚳蛙谏于王而不用，致[3]为臣而去。

齐人曰："所以为蚳蛙，则善矣；所以自为，则吾不知也。"

公都子[4]以告。

曰："吾闻之也：有官守者，不得其职则去；有言责者，不得其言则去。我无官守，我无言责[5]也，则吾进退岂不绰绰然有余裕哉？"

Mencius said to Qi Wa, "There seemed to be reason in your declining the governorship of Ling-qiu, and requesting to be appointed chief criminal judge, because the latter office would afford you the opportunity of speaking your views. Now several months have elapsed, and have you yet found nothing of which you might speak?"

On this, Qi Wa remonstrated on some matter with the king, and, his counsel not being taken, resigned his office and went away.

The people of Qi said, "In the course which he marked out for Qi Wa he did well, but we do not know as to the course which he pursues for himself."

His disciple Gongdu told him these remarks.

Mencius said, "I have heard that he who is in charge of an office, when he is prevented from fulfilling its duties, ought to take his departure, and that he on whom is the responsibility of giving his opinion, when he finds his words unattended to, ought to do the same. But I am in charge of no office; on me devolves no duty of speaking out my opinion: —may not I therefore act freely and without any constraint, either in going forward or in retiring?"

【注释】［1］蚳（chí）蛙：齐国大夫。［2］灵丘：

齐国边境邑名。士师：官名，管禁令、狱讼、刑罚等，是法官的通称。[3]致：归还，交还，此指辞职。[4]公都子：孟子弟子。[5]言责：献言之责。

【译文】孟子对蚔蛙说："您辞去灵丘的长官而请求去做法官，这似乎是正确的，因为这样可以（接近齐王）向齐王进言了。现在，您做了法官已经好几个月了，还不可以向齐王进言吗？"

蚔蛙向齐王进谏但不被采用，于是辞职而去。

齐国人说："孟子为蚔蛙的考虑似乎是有道理的，但是他自己在这个位置会怎样，我们就不知道了。"

公都子把齐国人的议论告诉了孟子。

孟子说："我听说过：有官位的人，如果无法行使其职责就应该辞去；有进言责任的谏官，如果无法尽到进言之责，就应该辞职。

至于我既没有官位又没有进言的责任，那么我的进退去留，岂不是非常宽松而有自由的回旋余地吗？"

【解读】本章的蚔蛙比上一章能悔过知错的孔距心要高明一些，不仅是一位知廉耻的君子，而且是一位懂得担当且知进退的官员。他在其位，谋其事，尽其职；做谏官，进言不被采纳，遂挂冠而去，留给历史一个潇洒的背影，让后人钦佩、思考、回味。不论是为官做宰，还是举言进谏，都应该以称其职为标准，以保住其尊严与人格，不应该以高官厚禄为目标，以致丧失尊严与人格。

4.6

　　孟子为卿于齐，出吊于滕，王使盖大夫王驩为辅行[1]。王驩朝暮见，反[2]齐、滕之路，未尝与之言行事也。

　　公孙丑曰："齐卿之位，不为小矣；齐滕之路，不为近矣。反之而未尝与言行事，何也？"

　　曰："夫既或治之，予何言哉？"

Mencius, occupying the position of a high dignitary in Qi, went on a mission of condolence to Teng. The king also sent Wang Huan, the governor of Gai, as assistant-commissioner. Wang Huan, morning and evening, waited upon Mencius, who, during all the way to Teng and back, never spoke to him about the business of their mission.

Gongsun Chou said to Mencius, "The position of a high dignitary of Qi is not a small one; the road from Qi to Teng is not short. How was it that during all the way there and back, you never spoke to Huan about the matters of your mission?"

Mencius replied, "There were the proper officers who attended to them. What occasion had I to speak to him about them?"

【注释】［1］盖（gě）：齐国邑名。王驩（huān）：齐王的宠臣。辅行：副使。［2］反：同"返"。

【译文】孟子在齐国担任国卿，出使到滕国吊丧，齐王派盖邑的长官王驩做孟子的副使。王驩早晚同孟子相见，在返回齐国的路上，孟子却从来没有与他谈起过此次吊丧的事。

公孙丑说："您作为齐国国卿，职位不算小了，从齐国到滕国的路程也不算近了。但您返回途中未曾与他谈过公事，这是为什么呢？"

孟子说："既然他已经把所有的事情都

包办了，我还有什么好说的呢？"

【解读】本章通过孟子奉命与王驩同行到滕国吊
丧后返回齐国路上，孟子不与王驩交流来表
明其态度。从孟子"夫既或治之，予何言哉？"
一语可知，他们在滕国之行并不愉快，原因
就在于王驩作为孟子的副使却恃宠越俎代庖，
独断专行。面对这么一个不懂礼数的粗鄙小
人，孟子不屑理会，故而沉默不言。孟子的
沉默，是对权奸的蔑视，也是对自己尊严的
维护。

4.7

孟子自齐葬于鲁[1]，反于齐，止于嬴[2]。

充虞[3]请曰："前日不知虞之不肖，使虞敦[4]匠事。严[5]，虞不敢请。今愿窃有请也，木若以美[6]然。"

曰："古者棺椁无度，中古棺七寸，椁称之。自天子达于庶人，非直为观美也，然后尽于人心。不得，不可以为悦；无财，不可以为悦。得之为有财，古之人皆用之，吾何为独不然？且比化者[7]，无使土亲肤，于人心独无恔[8]乎？吾闻之君子：不以天下俭其亲。"

Mencius went from Qi to Lu to bury his mother. On his return to Qi, he stopped at Ying.

Chong Yu begged to put a question to him, and said, "Formerly, in ignorance of my incompetency, you employed me to superintend the making of the coffin. As you were then pressed by the urgency of the business, I did not venture to put any question to you. Now, however, I wish to take the liberty to submit the matter. The wood of the coffin, it appeared to me, was too good."

Mencius replied, "Anciently, there was no rule for the size of either the inner or the outer coffin. In middle antiquity, the inner coffin was made seven inches thick, and the outer one the same. This was done by all, from the sovereign to the common people, and not simply for the beauty of the appearance, but because they thus satisfied the natural feelings of their hearts. If prevented by statutory regulations from making their coffins in this way, men cannot have the feeling of pleasure. If they have not the money to make them in this way, they cannot have the feeling of pleasure. When they were not prevented, and had the money, the ancients all used this style. Why should I alone not do so? And moreover, is there no satisfaction to the natural feelings of a man, in preventing the earth from getting near to the bodies of his dead? I have heard that the superior man will not for all the world be niggardly to his parents."

【注释】[1]自齐葬于鲁：孟子在齐做官，母丧，归葬于鲁。[2]嬴：齐国邑名，在今山东莱芜西北。[3]充虞：孟子弟子。[4]敦：督促。[5]严：急。[6]以美：太美。以：通"已"，太，甚。[7]化者：死者。[8]恔（xiào）：快慰。

【译文】孟子从齐国到鲁国安葬母亲，返回齐国时，在嬴邑停留。

充虞请教孟子说："前些日子承蒙您看得起，让我督管打造棺椁的工作。当时事急，我不敢向您请教。现在想请教您，棺木是不是有些太华美了。"

孟子回答说："上古对于棺椁的尺寸并没有一定的标准，中古时候才规定棺木厚七寸，椁的厚度与棺相称。从帝王到平民百姓，

讲究棺椁不仅仅是为了美观，而是必须这样
才算尽了孝心。为礼制所限得不到好棺木，
就不会称心；没有钱财，也不会称心。有地
位能使用好棺木且又有钱财，古人都选择好
棺木，我为什么单单不能这样呢？况且，这
样做不过是为了不让泥土挨着死者的尸体，
对于孝子之心岂不是一种慰藉吗？我听说过，
君子不会因为天下事而在父母身上节俭。"

【解读】孟母是天下贤母的榜样，她的三迁教
子闻名天下。如果没有孟母含辛茹苦地塑造
孟子的人格，就没有孟子成年后的一切。慈
母离世，做儿子的尽心送别母亲以表达孝子
之情，难道不是人之常情吗？孟子认为，在
财力允许的情况下，要求棺木做得好一些，
既合乎礼制，也尽了人子之心，并没有什么
不妥。孟子这里重在一个"孝"字，为母亲
做上等的棺椁是孝心的体现，依然坚守着礼
制与财力许可两大原则。

充虞问丧仪于孟子　卢冰　绘

4.8

沈同 [1] 以其私问曰："燕可伐与？"

孟子曰："可。子哙 [2] 不得与人燕，子之 [3]
不得受燕于子哙。有仕于此，而子悦之，不
告于王而私与之吾子之禄爵；夫士也，亦无
王命而私受之于子，则可乎？何以异于是？"

齐人伐燕。

或问曰："劝齐伐燕，有诸？"

曰："未也。沈同问'燕可伐与'，吾
应之曰'可'，彼然而伐之也。彼如曰：'孰
可以伐之？'则将应之曰：'为天吏 [4]，则
可以伐之。'今有杀人者，或问之曰：'人
可杀与？'则将应之曰：'可。'彼如曰：'孰
可以杀之？'则将应之曰：'为士师则可以
杀之。'今以燕伐燕，何为劝之哉？"

Shen Tong, on his own impulse, asked Mencius,
saying, "May Yan be smitten?"

Mencius replied, "It may. Zikuai had no right to give Yan to another man, and Zizhi had no right to receive Yan from Zikuai. Suppose there were an officer here, with whom you, Sir, were pleased, and that, without informing the king, you were privately to give to him your salary and rank; and suppose that this officer, also without the king's orders, were privately to receive them from you: —would such a transaction be allowable? And where is the difference between the case of Yan and this?"

The people of Qi smote Yan.

Some one asked Mencius, saying, "Is it really the case that you advised Qi to smite Yan?"

He replied, "No. Shen Tong asked me whether Yan might be smitten, and I answered him, 'It may.' They accordingly went and smote it. If he had asked me, 'Who may smite it?' I would have answered him, 'He who is the minister of Heaven may smite it.' Suppose the case of a murderer, and that one asks me, 'May this man be put to death?' I will answer him, 'He may.' If he ask me, 'Who may put him to death? 'I will answer him, 'The chief criminal judge may put him to death.' But now with one Yan to smite another Yan:—how should I have advised this?"

【注释】［1］沈同：齐国大夫。［2］子哙（kuài）：燕国国君，名哙。［3］子之：燕国相，专权独断。子哙让国君之位于子之，引起燕太子及大臣的强烈不满，导致燕国内乱。齐国乘机出兵，攻下燕国都城，杀掉子哙与子之。［4］天吏：代表上天管理人民的官员。

【译文】沈同以私人身份问孟子："燕国可以去讨伐吗？"

孟子说："可以。燕王子哙不应该轻率地把燕国让给别人，相国子之也不应该从子哙手里接受燕国。比方有这样一个人，你很

喜欢他，便不向国君上奏而私下把你的俸禄
和官位转让给他；而他呢，也没有得到国君
的任命就从你手上接受了俸禄和官位，这样
可以吗？子哙、子之私下互相授受的事和这
个例子有什么不同吗？"

齐国讨伐了燕国。

有人问孟子："（听说您）劝齐国讨伐
燕国，有这回事吗？"

孟子说："没有。沈同问'燕国可以讨
伐吗'，我回答说'可以'，他们就这样去
讨伐了。如果他是问：'谁可以讨伐他？'
我就会回答说：'只有天吏才可以讨伐他。'
比如现在有个杀人犯，有人问道：'犯人可
以杀吗？'我将回答说：'可以。'他如果问：
'谁可以杀他呢？'我将回答说：'只有法
官才可以杀他。'现在，以一个和燕国同样
无道的国家去攻伐燕国，我为什么要劝说他
们呢？"

【解读】本章从燕国国君子哙禅让事件为发端，沈同问："燕可伐与？"孟子回答："可。"别人问："劝齐伐燕，有诸？"孟子又矢口否认，似乎孟子在玩文字游戏。然而孟子所强调的是"孰可以伐之"的问题，这是一个根本原则。

首先，燕国不是燕王一个人的燕国，而是燕国百姓的燕国，而燕王子哙错误地把国君之位私自授给了相国子之，导致了燕国内乱。这是违背了礼制、破坏了政权传承秩序的行为，于国于民无利，故而孟子认为这种行为可以攻伐。

其次，孟子认为要讨伐不义的燕国，齐国不具备资格，攻打了燕国，齐国也就成了霸道之国，非王道之国。那么，谁有资格讨伐呢？天吏。天吏代表上天的意志去讨伐无道之君。孟子所说的"天吏"，似乎是指代表民意的正义之士。孔子在《论语·季氏》中说道："天下有道，则礼乐征伐自天子出；天下无道，则礼乐征伐自诸侯出。"天下事，无外乎一个规矩，一种秩序，不能想当然乱来，这就是那个时代的礼制。虽然《淮南子》说"燕子唅行仁而亡"，但在当时的时局下破坏了礼制，天下就会大乱。"春秋无义战"大概说的就是这种无序的乱象。

4.9

燕人畔。王曰：“吾甚惭于孟子[1]。”

陈贾[2]曰：“王无患[3]焉。王自以为
与周公，孰仁且智？”

王曰：“恶[4]！是何言也？”

曰：“周公使管叔监殷[5]，管叔以殷畔。
知而使[6]之，是不仁也；不知而使之，是不
智也。仁智，周公未之尽[7]也，而况于王乎？
贾请见而解之。”

见孟子问曰：“周公何人也？”

曰：“古圣人也。”

曰：“使管叔监殷，管叔以殷畔也，有诸？”

曰：“然。”

曰：“周公知其将畔而使之与？”

曰：“不知也。”

“然则圣人且有过与？”

曰：“周公，弟也；管叔，兄也。周公之过，
不亦宜乎？且古之君子，过则改之；今之君子，

过则顺之。古之君子，其过也，如日月之食，民皆见之；及其更也，民皆仰之。今之君子，岂徒 [8] 顺之，又从为之辞 [9]。"

The people of Yan having rebelled, the king of Qi said, "I feel very much ashamed when I think of Mencius."

Chen Jia said to him, "Let not Your Majesty be grieved. Whether does Your Majesty consider yourself or Zhougong the more benevolent and wise?"

The king replied, "Oh! what words are those?"

"The duke of Zhou," said Jia, "appointed Guan-shu to oversee the heir of Yin, but Guanshu with the power of the Yin State rebelled. If knowing that this would happen he appointed Guan Shu, he was deficient in benevolence. If he appointed him, not knowing that it would happen, he was deficient in knowledge. If the duke of Zhou was not completely benevolent and wise, how much less can Your Majesty be expected to be so! I beg to go and see Mencius, and relieve Your Majesty from that feeling."

Chen Jia accordingly saw Mencius, and asked him, saying, "What kind of man was the duke of Zhou?"

"An ancient sage," was the reply.

"Is it the fact that he appointed Guanshu to oversee the heir of Yin, and that Guanshu with the state of Yin rebelled?"

"It is."

"Did the duke of Zhou know that he would rebel, and purposely appoint him to that office?"

Mencius said, "He did not know."

"Then, though a sage, he still fell into error?"

"The duke of Zhou," answered Mencius, "was the younger brother. Guanshu was his elder brother. Was not the error of Zhougong in accordance with what is right? Moreover, when the superior men of old had errors, they reformed them. The superior men of the present time, when they have errors, persist in them. The errors of the superior men of old were like eclipses of the sun and moon. All the people witnessed them, and when they had reformed them, all the people looked up to them with their former admiration. But do the superior men of the present day only persist in their errors? They go on to apologize for them likewise."

【注释】［1］惭于孟子：孟子曾经劝齐宣王，而王不听，故惭愧。［2］陈贾：齐国大夫。［3］患：担忧。［4］恶（wū）：表示惊叹。［5］管叔：周武王的弟弟，周公的哥哥，封地在管。监：监督管理。［6］使：任用。［7］未之尽：不能全部做到。［8］徒：仅仅。［9］辞：设辞辩解。

【译文】燕国人背叛齐国。齐王说:"我对孟子感到十分惭愧。"

陈贾说:"大王不必担忧。大王您认为和周公相比,谁更加仁德有智慧?"

齐王说:"嗬!这是什么话!"

(陈贾)说:"周公派管叔去监管殷人,管叔却带着殷人叛乱。如果周公知道他会反叛还派他去,这是不仁;如果不知道他会反叛而派他去,这是不智。仁和智,周公还未能完全具备,何况大王您呢?请允许我见到孟子时向他做些解释。"

(陈贾)见到孟子,问道:"周公是怎样一个人?"

(孟子)说:"古代的圣人。"

(陈贾)说:"他派管叔监管殷人,管叔却带着殷人叛乱,有这回事吗?"

(孟子)说:"是这样。"

(陈贾)说:"周公是知道他会反叛而派他去的吗?"

（孟子）说："（周公）不知道。"

（陈贾说：）"圣人岂不是也会有过错吗？"

（孟子）说："周公是弟弟，管叔是哥哥。（谁能料到哥哥会背叛呢？）周公的过错，不也是合乎情理的吗？况且，古代的君子，犯了过错就改正；现在的君子，犯了过错竟将错就错。古代的君子，他的过错就像日食、月食一样，民众都能看到，等他改正后，民众都仰望着他；现在的君子，岂止是将错就错，而且还找理由为错误辩解。"

【解读】本章实际上在告诉我们齐国讨伐燕国的后果：齐宣王虽然已经知道了自己的错误，并且感到歉疚，但是不好意思面对曾经规劝过自己的孟子，可以说心胸不够坦荡。而陈贾却是一个地地道道地阿谀奉承之辈，正当齐王准备思过改正之时，他却要找些理由，拿周公当年"使管叔监殷"来说事，为齐王掩饰错误，让错误延续下去，阻止齐王改过迁善，实在是误国、误君之举，受到孟子含蓄地批评。其实，"金无足赤，人无完人"，犯错，在所难免。孟子认为，作为君子不在于犯不犯错，而在于怎样对待错误。古代君子的过错好像日食、月食一样，人民都能看到，等到他改正错误后，人民都会敬仰他；而后来的君子不仅将错就错，还要为错误做辩解，这种文过饰非的行为就像掩耳盗铃了。

4.10

孟子致为臣而归[1]。王就见孟子，曰："前日愿见而不可得，得侍，同朝甚喜。今又弃寡人而归，不识可以继此而得见乎？"

对曰："不敢请耳，固所愿也。"

他日，王谓时子[2]曰："我欲中国[3]而授孟子室，养弟子以万钟[4]，使诸大夫国人皆有所矜式[5]。子盍为我言之？"

时子因陈子[6]而以告孟子，陈子以时子之言告孟子。

孟子曰："然。夫时子恶知其不可也？如使予欲富，辞十万而受万，是为欲富乎？季孙曰：'异哉子叔疑！使己为政，不用，则亦已矣，又使其子弟为卿。人亦孰不欲富贵？而独于富贵之中，有私龙断[7]焉。'古之为市也，以其所有易其所无者，有司者治之耳。有贱丈夫[8]焉，必求龙断而登之，以左右望而罔[9]市利。人皆以为贱，故从而征之。

征商，自此贱丈夫始矣。"

Mencius gave up his office, and made arrangements for returning to his native state. The king came to visit him, and said, "Formerly, I wished to see you, but in vain. Then, I got the opportunity of being by your side, and all my court joyed exceedingly along with me. Now again you abandon me, and are returning home. I do not know if hereafter I may expect to have another opportunity of seeing you."

Mencius replied, "I dare not request permission to visit you at any particular time, but, indeed, it is what I desire."

Another day, the king said to the officer Shi, "I wish to give Mencius a house, somewhere in the middle of the kingdom, and to support his disciples with an allowance of 10,000 *zhong*, that all the officers and the people may have such an example to reverence and imitate. Had you not better tell him this for me?"

Shi took advantage to convey this message by means of the disciple Chen, who reported his words to Mencius.

Mencius said, "Yes, but how should the officer Shi know that the thing could not be? Suppose that I wanted to be rich, having formerly declined 100,000 *zhong*, would my now accepting 10,000 be the conduct of one desiring riches? Ji -sun said, 'A strange man was Zishu Yi. He pushed himself into the service of government. His prince declining to employ him, he had to retire indeed, but he again schemed that his son or younger brother should be made a high officer. Who indeed is there of men but wishes for riches and honour? But he only, among the seekers of these, tried to monopolize the conspicuous mound. Of old time, the market-dealers exchanged the articles which they had for others which they had not, and simply had certain officers to keep order among them. It happened that there was a mean fellow, who made it a point to look out for a conspicuous mound, and get up upon it. Thence he looked right and left, to catch in his net the whole gain of the market. The people all thought his conduct mean, and therefore they proceeded to lay a tax upon his wares. The taxing of traders took its rise from this mean fellow.'"

【注释】［1］致为臣而归：指孟子辞去齐宣王的客卿之职而归故乡。致，在古代有"致仕""致禄""致政"等多种说法，其中的"致"都是"归还""辞去"的意思。［2］时子：齐国大臣。［3］中国：在国都中，指临淄城。［4］钟：古代度量单位。［5］矜式：效法。［6］陈子：孟子弟子陈臻。［7］龙断：即"垄断"。［8］丈夫：对成年男子的通称。［9］罔：通"网"，网罗，搜刮，牟取。

【译文】孟子辞去齐国的官职准备回乡。齐王去见孟子，说："以前想要见到您却见不到，后来等到同朝共事我非常高兴。现在您又要弃我回家了，不知道我们以后还能不能像现在这样经常相见？"

（孟子）回答说："我不敢请求罢了，这本来就是我的愿望。"

过了几天，齐王对臣下时子说："我想在都城中送一栋房子给孟子，再用万钟粮食供养他的学生，使各位大夫和国民都有效法的榜样。你何不替我向孟子谈谈呢？"

时子便托陈臻把这话转告孟子，陈臻也就把时子的话告诉了孟子。

孟子说："嗯。那时哪里知道这事是不可以的呢？如果我是贪图财富的人，辞去十万钟却去接受一万钟，这是想要富吗？季孙曾经说过：'子叔疑真是奇怪！自己想做官，不被任用也就算了，却又让自己的子弟去做卿大夫。人谁不想富贵呢？可他却想在这做

官发财搞垄断。’就像古代的市场交易，本
来是用自己有的换取没有的，有关部门只是
管理这些交易罢了。但有这么一个卑劣的人，
一定要找一个独立的高地登上去，左右观望
想把全市场的利润都取为己有。人们都觉得
这人卑贱，因此向他征税。向商人征税就是
从这种卑贱小人开始的。”

【解读】孟子为推行仁政来到齐国，欲做齐王
之师、不召之臣，而齐宣王对孟子只是表面
上恭敬，实际上却不采纳他的谏言。出于无奈，
孟子要辞别回乡，而齐宣王考虑孟子的声望
对齐国还有用处，便以送房产、万钟粮为条
件相挽留。孟子不愿做供起来的菩萨，他既
不是为了求富贵来到齐国，更不是那种"左
右望而罔市利"的商人，他是为了实现自己
的政治抱负而来。如果自己的政治主张得不
到施行，"万钟于我何加焉？"

4.11

孟子去齐，宿于昼 [1]。有欲为王留行者，坐而言。不应，隐几而卧 [2]。

客不悦曰："弟子齐 [3] 宿而后敢言，夫子卧而不听，请勿复敢见矣。"

曰："坐！我明语子。昔者鲁缪公无人乎子思之侧 [4]，则不能安子思；泄柳、申详 [5]，无人乎缪公之侧，则不能安其身。子为长者 [6] 虑，而不及子思，子绝长者乎？长者绝子乎？"

Mencius, having taken his leave of Qi, was passing the night in Zhou.

A person who wished to detain him on behalf of the king, came and sat down, and began to speak to him. Mencius gave him no answer, but leant upon his stool and slept. The visitor was displeased, and said, "I passed the night in careful vigil, before I would venture to speak to you, and you, Master, sleep and do not listen to me. Allow me to request that I may not again presume to see you."

Mencius replied, "Sit down, and I will explain the case clearly to you. Formerly, if the duke Mou had not kept a person by the side of Zisi, he could not have induced Zisi to remain with him. If Xie Liu and Shen Xiang had not had a remembrancer by the side of the duke Mou, he would not have been able to make them feel at home and remain with him. You anxiously form plans with reference to me, but you do not treat me as Zisi was treated. Is it you, Sir, who cut me? Or is it I, who cut you?"

【注释】［1］昼：齐国邑名。［2］隐几而卧：指靠着几案睡眠。［3］齐（zhāi）：通"斋"，这里是斋戒的意思。［4］鲁缪公：即鲁穆公，鲁国国君，名显。子思：孔伋，孔子之孙。［5］泄柳：鲁缪公时的贤人。申详：孔子弟子子张的儿子。［6］长者：孟子自称。

【译文】孟子离开齐国国都，走到昼邑住宿。有个想为齐王挽留他的人，恭敬地坐着跟孟子说话。孟子不理会，靠着几案睡觉。

此人不高兴，说："我先斋戒了一夜，然后才敢来和您说话，但您只顾着睡觉而不听，今后恐怕再也不敢来见您了。"

孟子说："坐下！我明白地告诉你。从前，鲁缪公要是没有让人侍奉在子思身边，就不能使子思安心留下；要是没有贤人在鲁缪公身边，就不能使泄柳、申详安心。你为我这个长辈考虑，却不想鲁缪公是怎样对待子思的，这是你拒绝我这个长辈呢，还是我这个长辈拒绝你呢？"

【解读】本章通过孟子与齐国说客的对话，意在表明：尊重他人才是留住人心的最佳途径。孟子离开齐国并非己愿，他又何尝不想在齐国大展身手，使儒家仁政王道学说得以实施呢？只是孟子在齐国没有得到齐王应有的尊重。孟子以鲁缪公对待子思作比，意在说明如果无法实施王道仁政，无论鲁缪公对子思是何等的尊敬，也难以留住子思。而身边这个矫情的说客不能理解孟子的心情，所以孟子说："子为长者虑，而不及子思，子绝长者乎？长者绝子乎？"逻辑关系就是这样产生的。其实结合前几章通篇来看，孟子并非要在齐国获得什么礼遇，只要能够实现自己的抱负，齐王能够听取并采纳自己的建议，就是对自己最大的尊重。但齐宣王通过一系列的行径表明，他对孟子的态度不过是"叶公好龙"罢了。

4.12

　　孟子去齐。尹士[1]语人曰："不识王之不可以为汤、武，则是不明也；识其不可，然且至，则是干泽[2]也。千里而见王，不遇[3]故去。三宿而后出昼，是何濡滞[4]也？士则兹不悦。"

　　高子[5]以告。

　　曰："夫尹士恶[6]知予哉？千里而见王，是予所欲也；不遇故去，岂予所欲哉？予不得已也。予三宿而出昼，于予心犹以为速。王庶几[7]改之。王如改诸，则必反予。夫出昼而王不予追也，予然后浩然[8]有归志。予虽然，岂舍王哉？王由足用为善[9]。王如用予，则岂徒齐民安，天下之民举安。王庶几改之，予日望之。予岂若是小丈夫然哉？谏于其君而不受，则怒，悻悻然[10]见于其面。去则穷日之力而后宿哉？"

　　尹士闻之曰："士诚小人也。"

孟
子

When Mencius had left Qi, Yin Shi spoke about him to others, saying, "If he did not know that the king could not be made a Tang or a Wu, that showed his want of intelligence. If he knew that he could not be made such, and came notwithstanding, that shows he was seeking his own benefit. He came a thousand *li* to wait on the king; because he did not find in him a ruler to suit him, he took his leave, but how dilatory and lingering was his departure, stopping three nights before he quitted Zhou! I am dissatisfied on account of this."

The disciple Gao informed Mencius of these remarks.

Mencius said, "How should Yin Shi know me! When I came a thousand *li* to wait on the king, it was what I desired to do. When I went away because I did not find in him a ruler to suit me, was that what I desired to do? I felt myself constrained to do it. When I stopped three nights before I quitted Zhou, in my own mind I still considered my departure speedy. I was hoping that the king might change. If the king had changed, he would certainly have recalled me. When I quitted Zhou, and the king had not sent after me, then, and not till then, was my mind resolutely bent on returning to Cao. But, notwithstanding that, how can it be said that I give up the king? The king, after all, is one who may be made to do what is good. If he were to use me, would it be for the happiness of the people of Qi only? It would be for the happiness of the people of the whole kingdom. I am hoping that the king will change. I am daily hoping for this. Am I like one of your little-minded people? They will remonstrate with their prince, and on their remonstrance not being accepted, they get angry; and, with their passion displayed in their countenance, they take their leave, and travel with all their strength for a whole day, before they will stop for the night."

When Yin Shi heard this explanation, he said, "I am indeed a small man."

【注释】［1］尹士：齐国人。［2］干：求取。泽：恩泽，恩惠。［3］不遇：不得志，不被赏识。［4］濡滞：停留，迟延。［5］高子：孟子弟子。［6］恶（wū）：怎，如何。［7］庶几：也许，可能。［8］浩然：如水流不可止，势不可遏。［9］由：通"犹"，尚且。足用：足以，可以。［10］悻（xìng）悻然：怨恨失意的样子。

【译文】孟子离开齐国。尹士对他人说："孟子不知道齐王不能成为像商汤王和周武王一样的帝王，那就是不明白世事；知道他不能，但是还要来，那就是想要求取国君的恩惠。行走千里来见齐王，不被赏识就离开，在昼邑住宿了三天才走，为什么停留在那儿慢腾腾地不走呢？我对这种人不喜欢。"

高子把这番话告诉了孟子。

（孟子）说："尹士怎能了解我呢？不远千里来见齐王，是我希望的；得不到赏识而离开，这难道是我希望的结果吗？我是不得已啊。我住了三天才离开昼邑，在我心里还觉得快了，齐王如果改变态度，那必定会反过来找我。我离开昼邑，齐王没有追我，我这才下定了毅然归家的决心。我尽管这样做，难道是肯舍弃齐王吗？齐王还是足以施行仁政的。齐王如果重用我，我怎能只是让齐国的人民得到安康？天下的人民都能得到安定。齐王也许能改变对我的认知，我天天盼望着。我难道是那种心胸狭隘的男人吗？向国君进言不被接受，就发怒，怨恨失意的神色露在脸上，一旦离开非得拼尽力气后才肯停止吗？"

尹士听到这话后，说："我真是一个小人呀！"

【解读】本章让我们看到了两个真实的历史人
物:一个见识短浅、知错就改的尹士,一个
进退有节、欲伸大义于天下的孟子。尹士比
较世俗,但本性直爽,有话就讲,说不喜欢
孟子的做法就直来直去地表达了出来;当听
到孟子为天下苍生计的拳拳之心后,立马痛
心疾首,痛加贬斥于己:"士诚小人也。"
这让我想到了另一对历史人物——负荆请罪
的廉颇和"先国家之急而后私仇"的蔺相如,
同样让我们动容。

面对尹士的责难,孟子是细述心曲,自
己不远千里来到齐国,不是为了谋求富贵荣
华,而是想辅佐齐王成为汤武一样的圣王,
由安齐国之民到安天下之民。至于离开齐国,
是迫不得已的,到了边境有意留了"三宿",
是盼齐王能幡然醒悟,回心转意。历史给了
齐王一次仁行天下的机会,却被生生地错过,
只留下孟老夫子不见齐王来请而兴起"浩然
有归志",留下了毅然决然归去的落寞背影。

至于尹士说的齐王不能成圣的看法，孟子其实不以为然，他有着极强的自信，坚信"不为也，非不能也"，做圣王不是能不能，而是为不为的问题。

4.13

孟子去齐。充虞路问曰："夫子若有不豫[1]色然。前日虞闻诸夫子曰：'君子不怨天，不尤人。'"

曰："彼一时，此一时也。五百年必有王者兴[2]，其间必有名世者[3]。由周而来，七百有余岁矣。以其数则过矣，以其时考之则可矣。夫天未欲平治天下也，如欲平治天下，当今之世，舍我其谁也？吾何为不豫哉？"

When Mencius left Qi, Chong Yu questioned him upon the way, saying, "Master, you look like one who carries an air of dissatisfaction in his countenance. But formerly I heard you say, 'The superior man does not murmur against Heaven, nor grudge against men.'"

Mencius said, "That was one time, and this is another. It is a rule that a true royal sovereign should arise in the course of five hundred years, and that during that time there should be men illustrious in their generation. From the commencement of the Zhou dynasty till now, more than seven hundred years have elapsed. Judging numerically, the date is past. Examining the character of the present time, we might expect the rise of such individuals in it. But Heaven does not yet wish that the kingdom should enjoy tranquillity and good order. If it wished this, who is there besides me to bring it about? How should I be otherwise than dissatisfied?"

【注释】［1］豫：高兴。［2］五百年必有王者兴：朱熹《四书章句集注》曰："自尧舜至汤，自汤至文武，皆五百余年而圣人出。"［3］名世者：朱熹《四书章句集注》曰："名世，谓其人德业闻望，可名于一世者，为之辅佐，若皋陶、稷、契、伊尹、莱朱、太公望、散宜生之属。"

【译文】孟子离开齐国，充虞在路上问道："先生好像有点不太高兴。以前我曾听先生说：'君子不埋怨上天，不责怪别人。'"

（孟子）说："那时是一种情况，现在又是一种情况。（从历史上来看）每五百年就会有一位贤明君主兴起，这其间必定还有德业闻望名于一世者来辅佐。从周朝以来，到现在已经七百多年了。从年数来看，已经超过了五百年。从时势来考察，也应该是出圣贤的时候了。大概上天还不想平治天下吧，如果想平治天下，在当今之世，除了我还能有谁呢？我为什么不高兴呢？"

【解读】孟子的弟子充虞因为老师曾说过"君子不怨天，不尤人"，而今看到老师离开齐国有些不高兴，似乎产生了怨天尤人之情，表达了自己的困惑。孟子给出了"彼一时，此一时"的回答。面对不同的时势，遇到的问题也会不同，如果孟子面对个人的困厄与贫

孟子去齐　吴泽浩　绘

穷，是可以无怨无尤的，面对去齐平治天下的理想破灭这样的大问题，怎能不让人失落而怨天尤人呢？孟子的不高兴，是为百姓仍处于水深火热之中、天下依旧没有太平而不高兴。当然不高兴的情绪是暂时的，孟子坚信"五百年必有王者兴"，中国的历史也确实是在一治一乱、治乱交替的历史规律中不断演绎着。而孟子认为自己有幸生活在一个乱久思安、天下将统一的伟大历史转折时期，相信自己将会是那位"名世者"，他对此充满着乐观与自信，并且自豪地认为能担当"平治天下"这一重任。"当今之世，舍我其谁与？"既有着"铁肩担道义""以天下为己任"的历史担当，又有着"天将降大任于斯人"的豪迈情怀，还有什么不高兴的呢？

4.14

孟子去齐，居休^[1]。

公孙丑问曰："仕而不受禄，古之道乎？"

曰："非也。于崇^[2]，吾得见王。退而有去志，不欲变，故不受也。继而有师命^[3]，不可以请。久于齐，非我志也。"

When Mencius left Qi, he dwelt in Xiu.

There Gongsun Chou asked him, saying, "Was it the way of the ancients to hold office without receiving salary?"

Mencius replied, "No; when I first saw the king in Chong, it was my intention, on retiring from the interview, to go away. Because I did not wish to change this intention, I declined to receive any salary. Immediately after, there came orders for the collection of troops, when it would have been improper for me to beg permission to leave. But to remain so long in Qi was not my purpose."

【注释】［1］休：地名。［2］崇：地名。［3］
师命：师旅之命，指战事。

【译文】孟子离开齐国，临时居住在休地。

公孙丑问："做官却不接受俸禄，是古
时的规矩吗？"

孟子回答说："不是。在崇地，我见到
了齐王。退下来便有了离开的想法，我不想
改变这想法，因此就不接受俸禄。接着齐国
有战事，不可请求离去。所以久居齐国，并
不是我的意愿。"

【解读】此章表明了孟子在齐有着强烈的责任心
和道义感。本来，仕而受禄，天经地义，而孟
子坚守"无功不受禄"的底线，不苟且为官。"仕
而不受禄"，让我们看到了孟子不忘初心的君
子之风，这是属于彼时孟子独有的进退之道。

后记

　　"中华优秀传统文化书系"是山东省委宣传部组织实施的2019年山东省优秀传统文化传承发展工程重点项目,由山东出版集团、山东画报出版社策划出版。

　　"中华优秀传统文化书系"由曲阜彭门创作室彭庆涛教授担任主编,高尚举、孙永选、刘岩、郭云鹏、李岩担任副主编。特邀孟祥才、杨朝明、臧知非、孟继新等教授担任学术顾问。书系采用朱熹《四书章句集注》与《十三经注疏》为底本,英文对照主要参考理雅各(James Legge)经典翻译版本。

　　《孟子》(一)由刘岩担任执行主编;

王新莹、韩振、王明朋、杨光担任主撰；朱宁燕、朱振秋、刘建、李金鹏、束天昊、张勇、张博、陈阳光、尚树志、周茹茹、房政伟、屈士峰、高天健、郭耀、黄秀韬、曹帅、龚昌华、鲁慧参与编写工作；于志学、吴泽浩、张仲亭、韩新维、岳海波、梁文博、韦辛夷、徐永生、卢冰、吴磊、杨文森、杨晓刚、张博、李岩等艺术家创作插图；本书编写过程中参阅了大量资料，得到了众多专家学者的帮助，在此一并致谢。